PRAISE FOR
AVENUE MA

Michael Farmer

"Despite all of the creative and media transformation that has happened in the industry, advertisers are not growing. Mat Baxter – while he may not know the actual industry data – intuitively understood this problem and essentially focused Huge to put the marketing community at the center of his universe. The marketing community needs help. There's 1) sub-optimal decision-making due to a lack of data transparency, 2) inadequate measurement systems to optimize decision-making, and 3) technological complexity that has not been mastered by the marketing community. If Huge is able to do what it needs to do to put the client first, then that helps clear the path for optimizing outcomes."

Bob Liodice, CEO, ANA (Association of National Advertisers)

"Michael Farmer highlights what the most successful agencies know: creativity devoid of results for clients does not grow or sustain a business. This book provides an interesting deep-dive into one agency's exploration to deliver greater value to clients by productizing their approach."

Marla Kaplowitz, CEO, 4As
(American Association of Advertising Agencies)

"Talk of transformation is cheap. Real transformation is difficult and deep. How does a company shape shift, reinvent and do so while serving clients and ensuring financial and business success? Madison Avenue Makeover shows how one company, Huge, rearchitected and resculpted itself for the future — and how we can learn from Huge for our own reinvention."

Rishad Tobaccowala, Industry Strategist

"Madison Avenue Makeover provides a set of lenses on the forces that are reshaping the advertising agency business, the power of digital technology in upending yet another industry, and the legacy business models of historic competitors that make them vulnerable to new insurgents. Yet, it also is a real-time story of how Huge, part way through the journey, with the end still not clear, is trying to create a new model for the industry."

Chris Zook, Global Head of Strategy (Emeritus), Bain & Company

"A fantastically detailed book capturing many of the nuts and bolts of the agency business, paired with an illuminating description of one agency's attempt to evolve."

Brian Wieser, Principal, Madison and Wall

"Mat Baxter and Huge are in mid-journey and there are two possible storylines. In one case, a hero goes to a strange land, overcomes threats, learns important lessons, and turns the adventure into a success. In another possible version, the hero makes a mistake and causes a major undoing. We won't know for a few years, but I have a feeling that we'll hear a great deal about Huge's success – it should attract so much client demand that they may have to turn away business."

Tom Triscari, Industry and Media Strategist

"Madison Avenue Makeover *is a book of many dimensions. It is the story of Huge's effort to transform its business model; of Mat Baxter, the CEO who is leading the transformation; of TBMC, the consulting firm hired to guide the transformation; and of advertisers' need for stronger growth. Huge operates in a flawed world that thinks that agencies are all about billable hours — an easier subject than figuring out how to drive improved performance for clients. Is the industry willing to experiment and follow Huge's example? Is Huge's change too dramatic for holding companies?" An entire industry is at risk until key players adopt new strategies."*

Sabrina Traskos, Global Procurement Leader, AstraZeneca

"Huge's paradigm shift provides an exciting example for the advertising industry, even if others do not follow Huge's precise path for products and organization. The shift to "results for clients" gives ample room for much-needed experimentation."

Kristen Simmons, Chief Operating Officer, PeopleConnect

"Few observers of the advertising industry dig as deep into the operating details of the actual work as Michael Farmer. The story of Huge — its founding, early success, and transformational challenges — reveals great perspective on the complex realities of creating sustainable value for and from clients. Mat Baxter's journey is one to learn from. It's never easy to lead in an era of industry disruption, but the ones who enable true transformation of their business model spur innovation for all ... and make history in the process."

John Seifert, Global CEO (retired), Ogilvy

"A 'how to' for an industry asking itself 'what now?'"

Jon Bond, Agency founder and Industry Strategist

"The transformation of the advertising industry requires not just a change in practices, but a change in paradigm. In Madison Avenue Makeover, Michael Farmer follows one agency's journey from a services-centric to a product-centric business model. Farmer invites us to look under the hood of an agency that has completely reorganized around the concept of selling solutions instead of hours."

Tim Williams, Author, *Positioning for Professionals*

"Madison Avenue Makeover is a great read for marketers and agency leaders dealing with how to deliver improved results. With the entire industry talking about transformation, Michael had a front row seat during Huge's transformation. He makes what could be a dry story an interesting read. Now that we know what Huge has been doing, we all look forward to the news of more results."

Joanne Davis, President of Joanne Davis Consulting

"Madison Avenue Makeover is extremely thought-provoking and pragmatic. All of the required dimensions of a new agency model are included for the benefit for consumers, customers and advertisers. It is a must read book for marketers and global ad agency decision makers."

Christine Removille, Partner, Customer & Marketing,
Bain & Company

"*In* Madison Avenue Makeover *Michael Farmer has given us three stories for the price of one. The first story chronicles the amazing evolution of Huge from birth and growth to stagnation and transformation. The second story is about CEO Mat Baxter – a young media executive who mastered turnarounds in Australia and New York before taking on the creative transformation challenge of Huge. And finally, there is a third story much larger than Huge – a parable for all of us about how companies can shoot across the skies with blinding intensity only to burn out – before being resurrected and restored by the right leader, the right ideas and a committed top management team. It's a story that gives hope in these troubled times.*"

Jim Singer, Partner and Member of the Board of Directors, Kearney

"*Michael Farmer has written a vital new book. His last book,* Madison Avenue Manslaughter, *outlined the problems facing the ad industry. It made clear that the only way to succeed today in the advertising business was to embrace a paradigm shift in management philosophy and measurement of results. In* Madison Avenue Makeover, *through the example of Huge and their CEO Mat Baxter, Farmer shows us a powerful model of management bravery, organizational restructuring, and results-based focus that may lead to success today and tomorrow. This book is an inspiration. Agency CEOs ignore it at their peril.*"

Brian Sheehan, Professor of Marketing, Syracuse University

"This sequel to Madison Avenue Manslaughter *builds on Farmer's unprecedented opportunity to roll up his sleeves and apply* Manslaughter's *lessons to a real life agency eager to forge a more central, business-forward role. The true wizardry of* Madison Avenue Makeover *is that despite all the operational detail, Farmer's writing makes this a real page-turner. So it's not just essential reading, but a good read as well."*

Nancy Tag, Professor of Branding & Integrated Communications (BIC), The City College of New York

"Mat Baxter is a thought leader and industry innovator. His latest innovation at Huge could be his biggest and best yet, with the power to revolutionize the entire ad industry."

Darren Woolley, CEO of TrinityP3 Australia

"Michael Farmer has a grasp on the future of the ad agency business like few others. Madison Avenue Makeover *is the story of how one substantial IPG agency, Huge, with a new CEO at the helm, transforms itself from old to new, on a trajectory that many others will need to follow for the Gen Z world ahead."*

Jeffrey McElnea, Industry Consultant

For Jo Ann

Published by
LID Publishing
An imprint of LID Business Media Ltd.
LABS House, 15-19 Bloomsbury Way,
London, WC1A 2TH, UK

info@lidpublishing.com
www.lidpublishing.com

A member of:

businesspublishersroundtable.com

© Michael Farmer, 2023
© LID Business Media Limited, 2023

Printed by Severn, Gloucester
ISBN: 978-1-911687-64-1
ISBN: 978-1-911687-65-8 (ebook)

Cover and page design: Caroline Li

MADISON AVENUE MAKEOVER

THE TRANSFORMATION OF HUGE
AND THE REDEFINITION OF THE AD AGENCY BUSINESS

MICHAEL FARMER

MADRID | MEXICO CITY | LONDON
BUENOS AIRES | BOGOTA | SHANGHAI

CONTENTS

FOREWORD
BY CHRIS ZOOK

I first met Michael Farmer more than 40 years ago, during the early years of Bain & Company, a consulting firm where we both became partners. When we met, the company had only one office and fewer than 100 employees. Today it has nearly 20,000 employees in more than 70 offices around the world. This shared experience has become one of the best stories of business building and the challenges of sustaining profitable growth that either of us know.

As our careers progressed, Michael moved on to the world of advertising and media, while I stayed at Bain, as head of its global strategy practice. We both wrote books about the challenges of navigating industry transitions, and the predictable challenges of successfully building businesses for the long term.

In Michael's new book, *Madison Avenue Makeover*, I see the imprint of our shared experience with growing companies, as well as a fresh perspective on an industry struggling to transform itself, seen through the lens of one company attempting to define the leading edge of that journey. In this case, that company, Huge, is a medium-sized business focused on helping organizations make their advertising and digital investments as effective as possible, while stuck in an industry with aging business models and traditions that are not as focused on results as they should be. Again, I see shadows of our common past in the consulting business, where Bain & Company differentiated itself as an insurgent through its fresh approach to the pursuit of measurable economic full potential.

Certainly, one can cite many business books, including my own, that have studied industry transitions and sought the common success factors, or business laws of gravity, that ultimately separated the winners from the losers. Typically, this is done by analyzing competitors' histories and trajectories, searching for patterns and lessons. Rarely is it possible, as in a medical clinical trial, to follow a story from the inside as it unfolds. But in the case of Huge, and its bold CEO, Mat Baxter, that is what Michael has been able to do in this book.

Madison Avenue Makeover provides a set of lenses on the forces that are reshaping the advertising agency business, the power of digital technology in upending yet another industry, and the legacy business models of historic competitors that make them vulnerable to new insurgents. Yet, it also is a real-time story of how one of those insurgents, part way through the journey, with the end still not clear, is trying to create a new model for the industry.

That model shares common themes with insurgents in other service industries that were able to reshape the rules of the game in their respective arenas — deeper focus on the customer, new methods of measuring economic value, flat 'virtual' organizations designed to reinforce collaboration, and a self-conscious dedication to controlling complexity. This last element is important because, as I have discovered in my own research, and written about, complexity is the silent killer of profitable growth. Repeatable business models with these attributes are one way to reduce the chances of predictable crises of growth becoming fatal. Huge has crafted an approach that its leaders believe will allow it to focus on value creation, enable the entrepreneurial mindset so critical to the success of an insurgent business, and use the power of repeatability to reduce complexity.

Michael Farmer has provided a technicolor rendering of the first part of the movie, while the writers are busily working on the end of the script. It will be fascinating to see which ending the controllable forces of leadership and the uncontrollable forces of the world at large choose as the conclusion.

Chris Zook is a Bain & Company Partner (emeritus), the 20-year head of Bain's global strategy practice, and the bestselling author of The Founder's Mentality and four other books about strategic and organizational change.

INTRODUCTION

"You can speak freely – this is private beach."
Credit: Charles Barsotti / The New Yorker / The Cartoon Bank

Late on a Friday afternoon in mid-July 2021, with most Zoom screens extinguished for the day and sunshine predicted for the Northeastern US, many of us were planning outdoor weekend activities that would minimize the ongoing risk from Covid.

For baseball lovers, the Boston Red Sox had come to New York the previous day for the only scheduled major league game in the country, nominally kicking off a four-day series that Major League Baseball hoped would create some excitement in a sport that had been decimated by pandemic lockdowns. By late afternoon batting practice, though, New York Yankees players were walking off the field, and it was learned that three Yankees pitchers — all of them vaccinated — had tested positive for the virus.

None of this much mattered to me; I would stay put in Madison, Connecticut, where I had been living and working remotely since the beginning of the pandemic. There were worse places to be isolated, and I felt lucky. Madison is a quaint, 1950s-style town of 18,000 people on the Connecticut shoreline, halfway between Manhattan and Boston. It is too far from either city to be a bedroom community, but not so far away that commuting to New York by train a few times per week is out of the question.

We were with some friends at the local beach club. The sun was shining brightly, the water was inviting, and in our little corner of the world, all was well.

My mobile phone vibrated, and I pulled it out of my pocket to take a quick look at the caller ID. My screen said 'Mat Baxter.' I wandered off the premises — phone calls are frowned upon at the beach club — to take his call.

Baxter was the newly appointed CEO of Huge, a Brooklyn-based digital creative agency that was part of the Interpublic Group of Companies (IPG). This much I knew. Previously, he had been Global CEO of Initiative, the IPG media agency where I had been doing some work. Baxter was not my direct client, but we knew one another, and I had written him a note of congratulations on his Huge appointment.

Baxter got right to the reason for his call. "I have some thoughts about a writing project if you're interested," he said. "I read your book *Madison Avenue Manslaughter* and thought it was extremely interesting and insightful. It's a critique, though, not a guide. We need a guide that outlines a different business model for agency leaders. I've been at Huge for a month, and I see how much we need a new way of thinking about what the agency should do. We could work on a writing project together — you and Huge — while my management team is sorting out our future."

He went on about his new position. Covid restrictions had limited his ability to meet with employees, but he was talking with groups via Zoom and would soon have had direct contact with 1,200 employees in a dozen offices around the world. Huge was doing some interesting digital work, but too much of it seemed like short-term projects that were unlikely to have a major impact on client performance. "One of my thoughts is that we need to pivot from working on short-term projects to working in long-term relationships to help clients perform better," he said. "That will require an overhaul of the agency."

Later, I learned that Baxter was the fifth CEO at Huge since the beginning of 2018.[1] His predecessors struggled, failing to maintain growth. IPG had bought the agency in 2008, and its growth continued up to 2016, and then it flattened. IPG replaced CEOs in an effort to get things moving. Baxter, who'd had a positive impact on Initiative, the IPG media agency, had been talking with Philippe Krakowsky, the newly appointed CEO of IPG, about taking over the leadership of Huge. "I had been at Initiative for five years and in media for more than 20 years," he said, "and I was itching for a change. The opportunity came up to lead a creative agency, and I jumped at the chance."

Baxter was in the midst of getting to know his management team, which he characterized as a collection of strong individuals who could work together to define a new future.

He clarified that the guide he envisioned me writing would take the form of a book, and why he was talking to me about it. "Even if we do a book *together*, I want it to be your book, written in your voice. You're an industry expert and critic, and we're just feeling our way. It should include your criticisms of what we're doing. Otherwise, it will just be a book of propaganda, which I don't want. You're the right person to put together a guide and describe the good, the bad, and the ugly of our transformation. I want this to be an honest, professional book about our efforts. You will have the copyright for anything you write."

He concluded his pitch. "Think about it. If you're interested, let's get together soon and talk about how to make this happen."

I assured him that I was interested in the project, even though I didn't entirely grasp what Baxter was thinking. I could understand being a fly on the wall during their transformation, but I would be uncomfortable, as an inveterate consultant, standing by and reporting on any errors they were making. I would surely want to jump in to give them my advice. I could not understand how this could be a joint project — Huge would be 100% devoted to their own transformation. Did Baxter want me to write a guide and then document 'what happened,' once Huge executives tried to put the roadmap into action? This seemed close to his description of a book that would be written in an independent voice and include descriptions of mistakes, criticisms of ignored advice, and the good, the bad, and the ugly of an agency change program. But there was no time for me to write a handbook and then pass it on. If Huge was going to trans-form itself, they needed to begin immediately — they couldn't wait for a painstakingly researched and written guidebook.

We set a date for a long lunch and planning meeting in New York, where I'd have a chance to talk this through with him.

This was certainly an unusual situation — not only because it was about a potential book, but also because this was a conversation with a CEO who was thinking about the process of changing a creative agency by putting a new culture and mission in place.

I had been working as a consultant to the industry for many years, and although I'd had frequent contact with many senior executives, I was never on the receiving end of a CEO conversation about major change programs. This is not to say that the CEOs I worked with didn't understand the realities of the industry or the operational obstacles their agencies faced. Agencies have long been caught between fee-cutting clients and profit-hungry owners, and I sat in on many conversations about these issues. Never, though, did the discussions of industry challenges lead to the development of whole-sale change programs to overhaul operations.

This fact alone was surprising because during all my years at The Boston Consulting Group and at Bain & Company, I was used to see-ing corporate CEOs take vigorous action once they had the data and understanding of their companies' strategic difficulties. "We used to grow, and now we do not. Why? We need to do something about this." Or, "We used to be much more profitable, but now we are not. Why? We need to fix our profitability." The past always seemed easier and better performing than the present, but the difficulties of the present cannot be ignored; companies need new strategies to deal with new circumstances. These strategies lead to vigorous actions that were most often headed up by company CEOs.

I wrote about the industry in *Madison Avenue Manslaughter* in 2015, and in revised editions in 2017 and 2019, observing that fees for agency work were falling, workloads were rising, staffs were stretched, and employee compensation was depressed. Agencies were highly stressed operations whose working conditions were camouflaged by allusions to a glamorous, creative past that few living ad execs had actually experienced. The past pronouncements of David Ogilvy (1980s) were continuously invoked at Ogilvy, while DDB focused on Bill Bernbach (1960s and 1970s), and TBWA forever celebrated its involvement in Apple's Orwellian Super Bowl ad of 1984. No one was celebrating the industry's sayings or conditions of the past 15 years.

The prospect of writing a fly-on-the-wall book was daunting. I would need full access to Huge's past and present data, along with the freedom to conduct confidential interviews with the company's executives, including many interviews with Baxter himself. The idea of a joint writing exercise was a non-starter.

What if Baxter's leadership proved to be ineffective, or if clients were unwilling to deal with Huge in a different way? What if the expenditure of executive time and effort led to nothing more than an improved agency in a deteriorating industry? What if Baxter lasted no longer than his three most recent predecessors, who were appointed in 2018, 2019, and 2020? What if the executive team found my involvement a nuisance and asked for the book project to be terminated?

There were clearly some risks associated with the project, and they needed to be clarified before I committed to it. One thing I needed to do before moving forward was speak with a senior executive to get a more complete perspective on the company's situation. Baxter suggested that I talk to Mark Manning, who had been with Huge since 2018 and would soon be named Chief Operating Officer. He asked Manning to set up a Zoom briefing with me.

A few weeks later, in early August 2021, Manning and I spoke about his early thinking about the transformation. As he described it, Huge needed to set three key objectives: 1) change the way the agency *creates value* for clients; 2) change the way it *delivers value* to them; and 3) change the way it *monetizes value*. These objectives needed to be fleshed out, and Manning was involved in discussions with The Business Model Company, a consulting firm described later in this book, as a strategic partner to help define, validate and roll out the transformation.

In Manning's view, the transformation had to take place during the remaining five months of 2021 and over the entire 12 months of 2022 — 17 months in total. He would begin the process by organizing an agency performance audit, to establish Huge's starting point. That would be followed by a transition planning phase of three to five months, and then a transition rollout across the network during 2022.

Beyond this basic framework, he knew little about what the transformation might entail, and hoped that the performance audit would provide insights to help guide the rest of the work.

"We have never taken a global view of Huge's clients and work," Manning said. "We've looked at office performance when a given office was stagnant or unprofitable, but I can't recall ever doing this for the entire agency. We have, I think, 160 clients, and I cannot tell you what we do for any client other than the ones I work with directly."

He described the agency as a mini holding company overseeing its twelve independent offices, and each office was effectively a mini holding company for each of its clients. This needed to change, he thought.

After my discussion with Manning, I wrote a memo to myself — an early guess about Huge's situation and the shape of the transformation to come. These were my hypotheses at that early stage:

1. Huge, like most agencies, is a federation of offices and clients. Each of these relationships is managed in one way or another by Huge's Account Heads. The Account Heads are 'service-oriented,' giving each client what they want from their relationships. There is no uniform 'Huge Way' of defining the missions for these clients, no uniform way of describing the work to be done, no uniform way of structuring or documenting the work and no uniform way of determining fees. Huge accepts the work plan and fees proposed by its clients.

2. The Account Heads do their best, but they are not guided by an overall vision or agency modus operandi. They are guided by their clients, and this leads to a mélange of client management practices, good and bad scopes of work, attractive and unattractive fee structures, healthy and unhealthy productivity levels for individual client teams, and underperformance for the agency as a whole.

3. There are 160 different ways of doing business. Some of these are exceptionally good, and others are not so good. The overall outcome is suboptimal, even if Huge is better than its digital competitors. Huge is the product of its random ways of working around the world.

4. The transformation of Huge needs to be a top-down change program that affects the future performance and behavior of its Account Heads in their work with clients. The work needs to be charged out at higher rates, which is only possible if it generates measurable improvements in client performance.

5. The transformation should seek to convert Huge from a federation of individual clients, each managed in its own way, to a unified agency that has a clearly articulated way of doing business — each office will need to conform to *The Huge Way*.

6. The transformation should radically change the decentralized culture into a uniform, global culture.

My observations would prove to be only partly true. Baxter would take the Huge organization in directions I could never have imagined. The forthcoming transformation would be radical, dramatic and would require new management skills for its operation. At the same time, it would prove to be a visionary solution for the industry's challenges.

Would the transformation work? Who could know?

———————

In September 2021, sometime after Baxter and I had a three-hour working lunch to hammer things out, I signed a book-writing agreement that formalized his promise to give me the freedom to write an independent book. Our contract stated, in part: "Michael Farmer will have 100% editorial control over the chapters; provided, however, that those chapters will not reveal or rely on any non-public confidential information of Huge without Huge's prior written approval."

Thus, the company and I began a transformational journey that would stretch from September 2021 to October 2022. It was a fascinating process, viewed from the inside, as a highly committed CEO and his Executive Leadership Team (ELT) sought to: 1) develop a new vision for Huge's transformation, seeking a change from the 'client service model' that keeps many agencies from doing their best work; 2) put in place new products and a global organizational structure designed to implement the vision; 3) communicate with employees to condition them for the changes that were coming; and 4) identify the weaknesses or flaws in the new Huge that would require ongoing attention.

Baxter and the ELT were mindful throughout the transformation process, that there were no guarantees it would work. It was also unclear whether they would reach a point where they could say, 'We're done!" Successes would have to be fought for and created on a continuous basis. The management team brought to bear their best judgments about Huge's past and present, and made bets on the future, but knew they could not anticipate and plan for every eventuality.

The risks and uncertainties added an element of excitement to their experience, somewhat akin to the excitement (and fear) of heading into battle. Failure was not an option, but success was partly in the hands of Fate.

Follow along as Baxter and ELT carried out the transformation of Huge, dogged by the questions they could not shake: "Will this work the way it is supposed to? What more do we need to do?"

CHAPTER 1
HUGE — SUCCESS & STAGNATION

"I don't know. Somehow this was easier when we built their website."
Credit: Dennis Flad

Timing, vision, capability, and luck play their roles in the successful launch of a company. This was certainly true in 1999, when David Skokna and Sasha Kirovski, Serbian immigrants who had previously been high school friends in Belgrade, left their respective jobs to found Huge, a digital design shop, in the Dumbo (Down Under the

Manhattan Bridge Overpass) section of Brooklyn. Their first client was IKEA, which had worked with Skokna at the Deutsch agency, where he was creative director on the account. IKEA followed Skokna to Huge, where Kirovski, a former software developer at iXL Enterprises, joined him as the technology director for the client and co-founder of the new agency.

From today's perspective, it isn't easy to recall what the world was like a quarter-century ago, before the internet, e-commerce, and social media took over our lives. Websites had been in existence for only a short time, and they were still relatively unsophisticated. The look of sites was important to clients, and they hired agencies with strong graphic design capabilities. An early attitude was 'the web is print in a different form.' Printed catalogues were being replaced by online versions in what was viewed by catalogue retailers and automobile companies as an efficient, cost-saving measure. They were clearly easier to update than going through the process of designing, laying out, and printing hardcopy catalogues. Amazon was still in its infancy, selling books online for only five years at that point. Facebook and Twitter were still years away from being launched. Instagram would not appear until 2010.

Dumbo was a fringe section of Brooklyn, a scruffy, red-brick warehouse district in transformation, and Brooklyn itself was far from being the upscale hot spot for Millennials it is today. It certainly was not Manhattan in the eyes of the agency world.

Huge would have been easy to ignore were it not for the visionary thinking of its founders and their attention-grabbing work for certain clients.

Huge's work for IKEA focused on the Swedish furniture retailer's current website and its future online catalogue. The printed catalogue was the company's marketing foundation — a worldwide phenomenon that grew from 212 pages in 1979 to 384 pages in 1999, with more than 100 million copies printed that year. Potential customers registered online for a copy and the free catalogue was mailed to them. Your request included your email address, which the company used for marketing purposes.

IKEA's website was pretty bare bones in 1999.

IKEA'S 1999 HOME PAGE

Source: www.ikea.com, via:
https://web.archive.org/web/19990101000000/http://www.ikea.com*

You entered the IKEA home-page, selected a country, and were taken to a country site that gave you an online product guide, a directory of stores, an ordering form for the 2000 catalogue, a contact page for customer service, an information page about various aspects of the company, and a job application form. There was no online ordering capability.

Source: www.ikea.com, via:
https://web.archive.org/web/19991014003359/http://www.ikea-usa.com/content

The company would continue to produce printed catalogues for another two decades — a vestige of traditional marketing, with more than 200 million copies still printed yearly after 2010. By late 2020, IKEA finally announced that it was "turning the page on the catalogue and ending the print and digital versions."

By early 2001, driven by Huge's web work, customers could complete internet orders for IKEA products, searching by product category. The upgraded site map showed an extensive list of online capabilities:

IKEA US SITE MAP, WWW.IKEA.COM, MARCH 2, 2001

Source: www.ikea.com, via:
https://web.archive.org/web/20010302214322/http://www.ikea-usa.com/help/sitemap.asp

Huge pushed to extend the capabilities of IKEA's website. As Sasha Kirovski recalls:

Huge was moving very quickly in many new directions under David Skokna's strategic leadership, carrying out research and user testing, developing the commercial capability for online ordering and operational management. We were always thinking about how things might work in an online environment. We wanted to do more than make pretty websites. And people came to work for Huge because we began to do incredible projects. We created a culture that was based on our creative vision for the future of websites. We did not need to do any separate business development — clients came to us through word of mouth, from recommendations from existing clients.

Those early clients included CNN, Reuters, Four Seasons, Pepsi, Target, and JetBlue, which had been founded in 1999 as 'NewAir.' The JetBlue work was particularly significant — one of Huge's creative innovations involved putting the online reservation link up front on its home page, something no other airline had yet considered. Huge reasoned that potential customers visited the JetBlue site to learn about flights, research costs, and make reservations. Why not give them the purchasing capability up front, facilitating a more immediate sale without a lot of bothersome web navigation? Ease of purchase helped JetBlue differentiate itself from competitors, along with offering luxury seats with individual screens, plenty of legroom and in-flight entertainment from DirectTV® and Sirius XM radio.

The Huge-designed JetBlue homepage was elegant, simple, and highly functional.

JETBLUE'S HOMEPAGE ON MAY 10, 2000

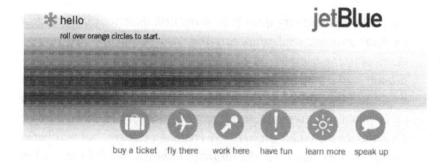

Over time, along with the groundbreaking work it was doing, Huge developed an edgy culture and image. Its executives were the iconoclasts from Dumbo who shook things up at their clients. The agency was growing rapidly, and Skokna and Kirovski strengthened the management team. They brought in Gene Liebel, head of project management at the Atlanta-based digital marketing and software company Silverpop, in 2002, and in 2005 they recruited Silverpop's founder, Aaron Shapiro, who'd been responsible for the company's growth, business operations and strategic leadership. Shapiro would later become Huge's CEO, leading the agency from 2010–2018. He would publish an influential 2011 book, *Users, Not Customers: Who Really Determines the Success of Your Business?* It made the insightful case that companies needed to do more than use the internet to chase customers — they needed to build a base of *users*, including employees and suppliers who develop online relationships with the company and its brands. Shapiro argued that relationship building must come *before* a company seeks to monetize its relationships with internet customers.

Ad Age selected Shapiro's book as one of the 'Ten Marketing Books You Should Have Read' in 2011.[2]

The agency's edgy culture and image were typified by the Huge Axe, a custom-made lumberjack's axe awarded to employees who reached their fifth employment anniversary. A photo of an axe-holder on the company's old website featured a heavily tattooed employee with the implement slung over his shoulder, looking as if he had just cleaned himself up after a particularly gruesome axe murder — the destruction of a client's traditional way of thinking and operating.

Huge had swagger as an organization, operating at the cutting edge of digital marketing and operations, expanding the concept of creativity by applying it to innovations in website structure and design, like its web work for JetBlue. Huge's leaders had a vision that digitalization would lead marketing away from its traditional vision — with its emphasis on images, sound, and words — and into a new realm where websites, software and revised operations would revolutionize and simplify purchasing and selling processes for clients and other users alike.

Huge attracted the attention of various suitors, and in 2008, nine years after it was founded, its owners sold 51% of the agency to IPG, with the remaining 49% held by partners Skokna, Kirovski, Liebel, and Shapiro. "Huge will have immense opportunities to partner with many of our clients and agencies to build brands into businesses grounded in experiences that are not only engaging, but also useful and productive," said Steve Gatfield, head of Strategy and Operations at IPG.[3] Huge then had 130 employees across its four offices, located in Brooklyn, Los Angeles, Atlanta, and London. Its sales were about $22 million at the time of the acquisition.

IPG invested heavily in growing Huge, and the agency opened new offices, turning each into a separately managed profit center under the leadership of an office president. Staffing and revenue grew rapidly between 2009 and 2016, increasing more than ten-fold by 2016, eight years after the acquisition.

Although Huge was a small player within the IPG portfolio, it became a 'feel-good' acquisition for the holding company. IPG shares were trading at an all-time low of $3.24 at the end of 2008, and the company hoped to build market confidence and bolster its stock price through this and other cutting-edge acquisitions.

Huge was a source of good news for the IPG leadership team. It was working as the digital vanguard for big-league clients. More importantly, there was something refreshingly pure and tough about the Huge operation. Its culture remained as creatively cool in 2016 as it had been when it was acquired in 2008.

The two original founders, Skokna and Kirovski, departed the agency in 2010, two years after the IPG acquisition. "This really has nothing to do with earn-outs or cashing out," Skokna said of his exit. "It has to do with time. I've spent more than ten years building this company. It's just time to move on."[4] Liebel stayed on to become Chief Strategy Officer, overseeing product design and analytics. Shapiro, who'd come on board in 2005 and became Huge's tenth employee, assumed the role of CEO in 2010. "The nine employees I met when I joined the agency are now running divisions of the company," he said, adding that he wasn't worried about maintaining the culture after it lost its founders, since many original employees remained in leadership roles.[5]

During its seven-year burst of growth under IPG ownership, Huge continued to publicize itself as a problem solver for clients. Its website became a repository of provocative think pieces that explored digital issues.

HUGE'S WEBSITE, MARCH 4, 2016

https://web.archive.org/web/20160304012221/http://www.hugeinc.com

"Real innovation is about solving problems, not just having ideas" stated one of these articles, arguing that companies should help customers figure out how to do things better. "There's always a way to make things faster, cheaper and easier. Start looking for problems that people complain about every day and take note of the little annoyances all around you." The piece also championed eradicating inefficiencies: "My corporate credit card keeps an accurate record of everything I buy for my company, but I still have to save annoying paper receipts for my expense reports." And it urged practitioners to take the initiative to solve their own problems.

Behind the scenes, though, Huge's work for clients was diversifying in countless directions, diluting the purity of the product approach that made it unique in the industry. The agency's product line was evolving toward traditional advertising services as each office, under pressure to continue growing revenues and margins, struggled to achieve growth.

The income statement was not a burden when Huge was growing organically between 2008 and 2016 — it then had a superior competitive strategy and digital practice, unlike any in the industry. The financial pressure became a burden when the agency's competitors wised up and began to position themselves in a similar manner.

Alex Pym, who joined Huge in London in 2016 as Vice President, Strategic Growth and Marketing in Europe, recalls his first year at the company, and the subsequent years, when its growth began to falter and there was extreme pressure from the Brooklyn office to win clients and add revenue at any cost:

Huge was never a truly connected global agency. It was a series of offices. From day one, we in London always had to go out and hunt for our own dinner, rather than benefiting from globalized support or growth from headquarters in Brooklyn.

Our legacy of digital user experience and design went from being a vast strength to becoming an over-serviced and heavily commoditized space. We expanded our sales approach in the US to include 'integrated marketing,' which was really traditional marketing, but client-agency dynamics were becoming worse rather than better, and this expansion of services resulted in less profitability.

One of the reasons that Huge's growth stalled is because there was too much focus on short-term financial results, and not enough focus on the successful outcomes we had been delivering to our clients. The integrated marketing services we offered did not make sufficient margins and did not really give us the growth we were seeking.

Martin Riley, who came to Huge in Singapore in 2014, after leaving Saatchi & Saatchi, thought that the agency had some undeniable strengths at first, but, over time, the business changed.

> *There was magic in the corridors at Huge. The senior leadership was very visible. They were hard at work, in the room with our clients. They were brutally honest. Our CEO at the time, Aaron Shapiro, would stand up in a room and deliver the most brutal assessment of a client's business. What he said was undeniable, and clients loved it. They loved the honesty of someone standing up to them, telling them what was wrong with their business — and what they could do to fix it.*
>
> *Later, though, we ended up trying to become a full service agency, and it was not the right path for Huge. We experimented, going into media, search and social, and chasing the money, which is never the right approach. And then we had so many different CEOs that our heads were spinning.*

The years 2016–2020 were stagnant, and revenue only picked up again in 2021, the second year of Covid, as it did for most of the advertising industry. During these no-growth years, IPG regularly changed the agency's CEOs.

Baxter arrived in 2021, looked at Huge's history and committed to revitalizing the company's strategy and reigniting its growth.

He hoped to reanimate Huge's global organization, which seemed to have lost its specialized competitive edge. It had become a service provider that undertook many different projects for a wide range of clients serviced out of twelve geographical offices. The organizational vibe remained, and axes continued to be awarded, but the swagger was more a remnant of past successes than a reflection of present-day cutting edge work.

To use a tired analogy, Baxter would have to rebuild the plane while it was flying. Although he did not lack confidence in his leadership ability, he had to admit that transforming a creative agency into something entirely new was not the same as overhauling media agencies, something he had been doing for the past 20 years.

CHAPTER 2
MAT BAXTER —
FROM ZENITH TO NAKED

Credit: Dennis Flad

Mat Baxter is, by his own assessment, an auto enthusiast 'gearhead,' obsessed with speed. As soon as he could afford to, he bought and drove fast cars, attributing this to a genetic link with his maternal grandfather, David Slingsby Ogle, a famous industrial and automobile designer who founded Ogle Design in the UK in 1954.

Ogle designed the Ogle SX1000, which incorporated a sporty fiberglass body, Morris Mini chassis and souped-up Mini engine.

During World War ll, Ogle had piloted a Supermarine Seafire, the aircraft carrier version of the iconic Spitfire fighter plane, operating in North Africa, the Mediterranean, and the south of France. He rose to the rank of Lt. Commander and was awarded the Distinguished Service Cross and named a Member of the Order of the British Empire.

Ogle was killed in 1962 while driving a racing version of the car, the Ogle Lightweight GT, to a British racetrack, where he was scheduled to showcase the vehicle.

Ogle's two sons, Baxter's uncles, remained involved with racing, and as a child, Baxter was fascinated by sports cars. His father took him to the London Motor Show in 1987 and sat him behind the wheel of a black Ferrari 328 GTB that was on the show stand, surrounded by a ring of red Ferraris. His father took a photo of his son behind the wheel of a Ferrari at age nine — and Baxter was hooked.

Fast cars and motorcycles are ongoing obsessions for Baxter, and he has owned a few, but it is not just the thrill and risk of speed that turns him on. He put it this way:

Designing an ordinary road car to reach 150 miles per hour is pretty easy. Any car manufacturer can do this. Building cars to go to 180 is a bit more difficult. But pushing that last 5% to 10% to get to 200 is disproportionately more difficult. Eking out incremental gains of performance above a certain threshold is complex and expensive, so there's a huge engineering gap between cars that go 180 and those that can go 200. You have to be so much better at engineering, body design, suspension, braking, manufacturing, and all the other things. Thousands of factors come into play for that last 5%. What separates Ferrari, Lamborghini, and Bugatti is that they do not stop at good. They go for great, and they put in incredible effort and investment to get the extra 5% to 10% needed for perfection. That's what separates the average from world-class players. I love sitting behind the wheel of a car where the manufacturer was not satisfied with 'good.' I want to know about companies that have gone all the way to 'perfect.' This goes well beyond car manufacturing. This kind of perfection should be sought in every industry.

When he became CEO of Huge, at age 43, Baxter was a newcomer to creative agencies, having worked for more than 20 years on the media side — at Zenith, Naked, Mediacom and UM in Australia, and IPG Mediabrands and Initiative in New York. He had an exciting and controversial career in media.

Mathew David A. Baxter was born in Surrey, England, in 1978 and grew up in the UK. When he was twelve, his parents decided that London was not the best environment for kids to grow up in — they viewed Australia as a better place to raise their son and two daughters. So, the family immigrated to Australia in 1990, and Baxter grew up Australian in Sydney, enduring the taunts of classmates who made fun of his 'pommy accent' for his first two years in high school. "It was pretty rough at first, but after a few years I began to fit in. People still say that I have a twang of British in my accent, particularly when I'm under stress, so if that's what you hear, you'll know what I'm feeling."

He went to Barker College, a private school in New South Wales, 25 km northwest of Sydney, where he stood out as a British new-comer for his first two years as a day student. Later, as a boarder — and more integrated as an Australian — he became head boy and was voted president of the student council. He knew everybody and was on good terms with most of his fellow students. "I had appeal across the board, which was something that allowed me to win the student council position. I was somebody who everyone could vote for and not feel bad about it." He did well in the humanities, and loved languages and history, but acknowledges being terrible at math and science.

At university, Baxter studied for a double degree in marketing and law. He was particularly fascinated by law, thinking that it would provide for a nicely delineated 'black and white' career — embodying the unambiguous notion of right and wrong, which was something that interested him.

"I wanted clarity in my life, and I thought that law and criminal justice would give me this clarity," he said. "I wanted certainty from my efforts. But very quickly I discovered that's not the way that law and the justice system work. The right side does not always win. You can only be as good as the 12 jurors making a decision, and they are all people with their biases and foibles. It was not as clear as I expected, so I dropped out of university and decided that I wanted to pursue a career in marketing instead."

Baxter began his job search by opening the classified sections of local newspapers and scrolling through what he characterized as the "famous names that might ring a bell" in the marketing and advertising game. This was, of course, before online job searches were a possibility. The television networks at the time were advertising for sales assistants — people to sell ad time to businesses. One of these was Nine Network, a high-profile Australian TV network. Baxter applied and was interviewed for a media sales assistant position. He didn't get the job but was referred to the media department at Saatchi & Saatchi, which since the late 1980s was run as part of the independent media company Zenith Media. It was an assemblage of the media departments of Saatchi, BSB Dorland, and KHBB in the UK. Media was going through a transformational period, coming into its own as an independent craft, liberated from the creative agencies to which it had long belonged.

Mike Boyd, Zenith's Australian Media Manager, hired Baxter for his first industry job in 1998, at the age of 20, just after Baxter had dropped out of university. Boyd recalled the young man he took a chance on:

For all of Mat's bravado and bullshit, and there's plenty of that, he's exactly the same today as when I first met him 25 years ago. Zenith was new, and I was responsible for media planning and buying for a large insurance company. It was a very laborious job. We were thinking, 'Let's hire a young assistant who can help us with the day-to-day, just to keep everything on the straight and narrow and chase any issues that come up.'

Mat was hired and he learned things very, very quickly. It was phenomenal how rapidly he could just pick things up and understand who the right person was to talk to, the way to deal with him, what was needed to get things done. And he just got it done and then moved on the next thing. This was absolutely fantastic and made him a standout — a quicker study than anyone else we hired in those days.

Mat was a risk-taker from the first day he came to work for me. He had a high degree of confidence in his own abilities. When you match confidence with attitude and aptitude, you have the makings of a habitual risk-taker. And Mat was, and I think still is to this day, a risk-taker.

Don't get me wrong, some of his risks fucked up magnificently. But even the ones that blew up in his face he would chalk up to learning, dust himself off and move on. No guilt whatsoever. He'd just move on.

He was a gigantic pain in the arse for some people — actually, for a lot of people. I mean, Mat was just one of these guys who would do things differently. I loved him because of that attitude. He was on people's wrong side, their bad side, more often than he was on their good side.

He never crossed anyone maliciously. He would annoy people rather than make people dislike him. He'd ring you at three o'clock on a Friday afternoon saying, 'I haven't got that booking confirmation.' I'd tell him to let it go. It was Friday afternoon, and the sales reps would be into their 15th beer at the local pub. He'd say, 'I don't care, give me their phone numbers. Which pub are they in? I'll walk down there and get it myself.'

He was relentless. He's just one of those people who is polarizing. You either love him or loathe him. He has a degree of passion that either drives the people around him crazy or super motivates them.

In Australia, the media-independent trend was initiated by Harold Mitchell, who left the creative agency Masius in 1976 and established Mitchell & Partners, Australia's first standalone media agency. In his 2009 autobiography, Mitchell outlined the compelling logic for media independence:

In the advertising industry ... methods were set in stone. A company with a product to sell often left all of its marketing to the advertising agency. The advertising agency was the centre of all power.

It was a time when the creatives and the account executives ruled from their glamorous offices. Way down below them were the media buyers — who didn't have big expense accounts or prestige or indeed much power.

I would get three minutes at the end of a two-hour meeting to explain how the advertising agency's money was being spent. I didn't think that was right. We might spend $50,000 on creating an ad and $950,000 on spending in the media. And most of the meeting would have been spent [talking about] the $50,000.[6]

There was more going on in the media business than the creation of newly competitive media independents. The agency compensation system was up for grabs. Traditionally, the full-service agencies were paid a commission from the client's media spend. That more than covered the agency's costs for the creative development of ads, media planning and buying, agency overhead, and the generation of profits. Once media services were spun out of the creative agencies (as at Zenith) or developed independently (as at Mitchell & Partners), the newly independent media agencies had choices: continue to be paid on media commissions, albeit at a lower rate (since there were usually no creative development costs), or negotiate fixed rates or retainers for media services. There were no set rules about this; an independent media agency could charge commissions with one group of clients and fixed fees for others. In the meantime, the full-service agencies scratched their heads over the disruption, wondering how to respond, but they were reluctant to kill the commission system, which was lucrative for them.

Baxter was dropped into this turbulent media environment in 1998, and he remained in media for the next 23 years, until he was appointed CEO of Huge. He had this to say about the experience:

I was incredibly lucky to live through those formative years of media coming into its own as a craft. I also observed that whilst media had freed itself from the day-to-day control and geographies of its former creative brethren, it had not freed itself from its faulty business model, which continued unchanged. Instead of saying, 'OK, we're spinning out, and we have a chance not only to right the wrongs of not being independent — of not being viewed as valued as the creative department — but we can also break out of the many other things that are broken.' The defects of the commission system loom exceptionally large in this respect.

The commission system rewarded agencies when clients spent money on the most expensive media channels, which were simple to plan and service. This created a bias for media agencies to skew their buys toward TV, and to soft-pedal or downplay other media solutions, like digital and social channels, which entered the picture after 2004.

Clients were complicit in this bias toward TV. They were motivated to spend the least amount of money and get the biggest bang for it, and traditional channels fit the bill. Digital and social, once they were introduced, seemed expensive because they were more nuanced and complicated to plan and implement. A million-dollar TV plan took less time to plan and implement than a million-dollar digital plan. Media agencies sought higher commissions for doing digital planning and buying, and were unenthusiastic about these emerging channels, which were complicated to manage and remained outside of their traditional areas of expertise.

As a junior strategist and media director on various accounts at Zenith, Baxter observed the channel biases of his senior colleagues and clients, and thought it was crazy. "Everywhere I looked, I saw media agencies and their clients stuck with legacy thinking," he said. "I was excited about new media and saw the biases against it."

Baxter developed a reputation as an outspoken troublemaker at Zenith Media. He was opinionated and tended to push against the traditions that existed in the agency. His colleagues saw him as just plain rebellious. He felt that Zenith should look at every media planning decision from a neutral perspective and recommend the solution that was right, rather than one that was most convenient or lucrative for the agency. He felt that there were right and wrong media choices to be made, and observed senior colleagues making all the wrong choices. Most importantly, he felt that an agency needed to be less self-serving and more client-centric.

He worked at Zenith for six years, mastering the strategic and operational complexities of media, and he was passionate and hard-working. Still, he felt the same kind of dissatisfaction he'd experienced as a law student — wanting to be on the right side of choices rather than living in an ambiguous world of compromises, flawed thinking and imperfect outcomes.

In 2004, when he was 26, Baxter received an unexpected call from John Harlow, one of the founders of Naked Communications, a groundbreaking creative and media-planning agency founded in London in 2000. Naked was turning the industry on its head by being channel-neutral rather than merely focused on traditional media. The agency was committed to providing objective strategic and creative advice for clients who wanted to do things differently. Naked sought out 'brilliant misfits' who could work in the agency's culture, where media strategy was seen a creative discipline in its own right. Naked charged fixed fees rather than commissions for its creative work and media planning; the actual media buying was managed by other agencies.

"Mat Baxter?" asked Harlow. "Mike Wilson told me about you." Naked was interested in establishing an office in Australia, and Wilson, one of the partners-to-be, wanted Baxter to join as one of the founders, along with Adam Ferrier, a psychologist and former strategic planner at Saatchi & Saatchi Advertising. Wilson, a British transplant to Australia, was at the time running the Sydney office of MEC, a WPP media operation.

The two met for a drink at a local pub, and Baxter accepted Harlow's employment offer. In the meantime, Baxter did some research on Naked. "I realized just how much of a misfit Naked was in the UK. They struck a chord with clients by being channel neutral — something that other media agencies were not. The more I learned, the more I saw Naked as an opportunity to get out of the very established, conservative media agencies. I quit Zenith and moved to Naked."

Ferrier described the early days of Naked in Australia:

I was the smart one, Mike was the nice one, and Mat was the crazy one. Mat would drive the business, Mike would look after the people, and I would look after the product.

We started the business straight away together, and within a couple of weeks, Mat and I were screaming at each other, yelling and arguing incessantly. At first there were only three of us, and this was fine. We were just business partners trying to form a relationship. But as the business grew and we started to have 30 employees around us, Mat and I were still having full-on arguments over silly things like the furniture in the office or the office wallpaper. Or, it would be about clients and the type of work we wanted to do and what type of ideas would be better.

Mike would come up to us and say, 'Guys, you've got to find a better way of working together because you're actually scaring the staff.' That hit home for us, and we eventually found a much better working relationship. He fast became an inspirational, supportive and loyal business partner, although part of our working well together was my having to realize that he was the boss.

Mat was very much the 'work hard, play hard' type of leader, and he dragged the agency into a rebellious mindset. It was us against the industry, a big fuck you to everyone, and the more we misbehaved towards outsiders, the better. Internally it was liberating and created an amazing culture; externally we were just seen as 'up ourselves twats.'

I remember he tried to sue News Corp — Rupert Murdoch — sending them a legal letter threatening to sue them for $10,000, and they wrote back saying, 'Do you know who we are? Fuck off.' I thought that was quite funny and brazen of him, but of course fruitless. However, it was about driving a need for clients to respect us as their agency partner.

Naked Australia, with Baxter, Ferrier, and Wilson as the agency leaders, was an astounding commercial success in that country, for a few years at least, winning Coca-Cola, Telstra, Absolut Vodka, and other major brands. "We were seen as troublemakers," said Baxter, "but in the backwards media industry, troublemaking meant doing things the right way. That's how screwed up things were elsewhere. We were particularly successful in stealing big media clients from WPP's media operations, and this infuriated WPP, but they were conventional, and we were a bunch of crazy guys who saw the media world differently. The whole premise of Naked was its swagger, its street-ruler type of attitude, its craziness. We were the lunatics who were let loose in the asylum. We would do crazy shit that nobody else would ever consider doing, and clients loved us for it."

One of Baxter's notorious stunts in January 2009 involved the launch of a men's store by Australian fashion brand Witchery. Naked was behind the creation of a fake YouTube video, *Man in the Jacket*, narrated by 'Heidi,' a distraught young woman who claimed to be trying to find the man who left his Witchery jacket behind in a café — a modern-day Cinderella story in reverse. Heidi, a convincing actress, duped a number of watchers into thinking that her situation was real, and that she really needed to find this guy. The campaign was soon exposed as marketing fakery, and there was a wave of media and social criticism over this 'unethical manipulation' of the public.

Amid the backlash, Baxter doubled down, loudly defending the campaign in the press and paying for market research that showed that it was extraordinarily successful for the client. As reported by *Mumbrella*:

> *Baxter had a message for the many marketing commentators who criticized the campaign. He said: 'We're aware of the hypothetical rules in this sphere — there are a lot of people out there who claim to have a rule book. But the reality is that it will be shaped by what the consumer will tolerate.'*
>
> *He added: 'We care about delivering for the client. If the industry is not happy, guess what? That is not a concern to us. I'm used to us being slagged as an agency. I was disappointed but not surprised.'[7]*

One month later, in February 2009, the global Naked agency was bought by the Photon Group of Sydney for $33 million, plus deferred payments tied to performance targets. The deal was reported to involve a four-year earn-out package for the agency's founders, with future payments dependent on Naked hitting growth targets between 2008 and 2011. Baxter had provided the introductions that led to initial discussions between Proton and Naked, so he was entirely knowledgeable about the acquisition.

Photon was a marketing services holding company, with divisions specializing in strategic intelligence, integrated communications, internet marketing/communications, and specialized communications. Photon saw Naked as entrepreneurial, fiercely independent, and challengers of conventional thinking, making it what they called a "natural fit for Photon."[8]

Naked, for its part, announced that the acquisition would allow the shop to "continue to pursue its vision, backed by the resources of the wider group."[9] Further international expansion was definitely in the cards.

However, Photon and Naked would have to carry on without the executive services of Baxter. He and Photon parted company shortly after the acquisition closed.

CHAPTER 3
MAT BAXTER — FROM AUSTRALIA TO NEW YORK

"Crikey! I brought the wrong backpack!"
Credit: Dennis Flad

Eight years after the 2009 acquisition of Naked by Photon, Naked shut down in 2017. It had been unable to maintain its growth, hobbled partly by Photon's financial difficulties, which were driven by excessive debt and too many acquisitions in too short a time. Naked found itself painted into a corner and inhibited by intense competition in the media agency space.

Naked's competitors had finally wised up and imitated the agency's approach to channel-neutral planning. "Market forces ensured that Naked's moment was a passing one. The other media agencies improved their strategic capabilities, and gave it away for free," wrote Tim Burrowes in a *Mumbrella* article headlined, "Naked Communications faces the sad fact that being clever doesn't make money anymore."[10]

After a six-month sabbatical in 2009, Baxter was hired by Toby Jenner, CEO of Mediacom Australia, the WPP media operation originally established by Grey Advertising. He was named Chief Strategy Officer, working with Jenner, who charged Baxter with "making Mediacom a winning shop in Australia." By his own account, Baxter expanded the job and "meddled in every aspect of Mediacom's operations." He remained there for just 18 months. This is how he characterized the experience:

> *During my tenure, I made my job bigger than it was meant to be. I thought: now that I'm the Chief Strategy Officer, I'll be in charge of many things, including the interior design for the office. So, I renovated the office, redesigned the way it looked, changed the signage, changed the branding, changed the templates for client presentations, and changed the way we recruited people. Anything that was important in the businesss, about brand, talent, or product, had to go through me. I was really a bit of a tyrant about this. In order to transform Mediacom, which was set in its ways as an old-school media agency, I had to shake everyone out of their comas and be completely disruptive.*
>
> *And so, that's what I did. But to be honest, I was only 31 years old, and I had never done a turnaround before. I was clueless about what it actually took to take an old-school agency and change the culture and organization. There were no textbooks or recipes. I just followed my instincts, and everywhere we saw a problem, we set out to fix it. That's how we went about making Mediacom a winning shop. I meddled in everything during the time I was there, in 2009 to 2010.*

Jenner and Baxter were credited with rapidly turning around Mediacom, which grew to be the number one media agency in Australia, becoming the most awarded media agency in 2010. In 2011, Jenner was named Australasia Agency Head of the Year.[11]

In 2010, Baxter was offered an opportunity to become CEO of UM (formerly Universal McCann), IPG's major media agency in Australia. Behind the scenes in his recruitment was Henry Tajer, an Australian wunderkind who had previously held the UM job in Sydney and was now in a senior media executive position with IPG in New York. Tajer was on the lookout for talented Australian executives.

Baxter took the UM job in Sydney in 2010 and remained there until 2015. He followed the playbook that had worked so well at Naked (do the right thing for clients) and Mediacom (meddle in everything and fix the problems you find). As CEO at UM, he found it easier to meddle than when he was Chief Strategy Officer at Mediacom — he did not have to assume powers that weren't formally part of his job description. What was new at UM was Baxter's strategy to strengthen top management through terminations, resignations and the recruitment of new executives.

In his five years at UM, he created a robust management team and a market perception that the agency was significantly stronger and more competitive in the Australian and Asian markets than it had been when Baxter first arrived. As evidence of this, in 2014 UM Australia was voted Agency of the Year at the Festival of Media Global Awards — the result of its performance across all the awards categories. It also won the Australian government's Cross The Line (XTL) anti-violence campaign's Gold for Best Social Media Strategy; Gold in the Best Entertainment Platform category; Silver in the Utility/Public Service category; Silver for Best Communications Strategy; and Bronze for the Best Targeted Campaign.

In 2015 Baxter was asked by Henry Tajer to move to New York and work under him as Global Chief Strategy and Creative Officer of IPG Mediabrands, IPG's media holding company. Tajer was at this point Global CEO of IPG Mediabrands, tasked with modernizing the group's media strategy. As reported in the Australian financial press in 2016:

For the previous nine years Tajer had led a bold diversification strategy at Mediabrands in Australia, extending its role beyond simply buying media space to making brand-funded documentaries and devising less traditional forms of advertising on the smartphones and tablets that have revolutionized not only how we consume media but how we interact with each other.

The big bosses at IPG wanted him to replicate this success globally from advertising's spiritual home, in and around Madison Avenue, from which the hit TV show Mad Men got its name. Tajer was in agreement that nothing less than a radical reinvention of the global game was needed.[12]

The Australian trade press covered Baxter's move with excitement. It saw Tajer leading an Australian take-over of New York's media industry, at least at IPG, and now Baxter was joining him. An article in *Mumbrella* was headlined, "Now that Mat Baxter has signed on for the project, Henry Tajer's Entourage is complete." It explained:

Baxter is the sixth senior Aussie exec to be joining Henry on his American adventure. Other than the fact that the boys from out of town are heading to New York rather than LA, the parallels with sitcom Entourage are uncanny.

As the leader of the pack, Tajer is clearly the Vinnie Chase of the team.

And now he's joined by door-kicking loudmouthed agent Ari Gold in the guise of Baxter.[13]

IPG Mediabrands owned UM, Initiative and BPN Network, its three media agencies; Reprise, its performance management (customer acquisition) agency; Magna, its strategic intelligence data agency; Rapport, its out-of-home (OOH) media planning agency; and Orion, its bartering company. Baxter found himself one organizational level above these stand-alone agencies, expected to influence and improve their performance through negotiating annual 'stretch' performance plans with revenue growth and margin targets; helping them win new business; reviewing their overall corporate strategies and organizations; and otherwise working as an influencer — without much real power — to help them meet their numbers while improving their performance. He found the experience like being a pilot who loves flying, but works in the control tower of an airport and communicates via radio with pilots who actually fly planes.

Initiative, which was part of his media agency portfolio, was not a sterling performer in 2015–2016, and IPG's perception was that it was not going anywhere, despite Tajer's and Baxter's attempts to influence its performance from the center.

Baxter and IPG came to the same conclusion about what Initiative and Baxter both needed — Baxter should leave his senior staff position at IPG Mediabrands and become the CEO of Initiative, with the clear understanding that the agency needed to be turned around.

And so, Baxter moved to Initiative in 2016, and recruited a new senior management team. He brought in Stephen Burford, who he knew from UM Australia, as his Chief Strategy Officer. Burford was then working for IPG Mediabrands in London, as Chief Strategy Officer for Europe, Middle East and Africa. Baxter elevated Amy Armstrong from BPN Network, which she was then leading, to become Initiative's North American CEO. Subsequently, they folded BPN Network into Initiative, reducing IPG's media agency portfolio to two agencies from three, and significantly expanding Initiative's organization and global scope.

IPG's current CEO, Philippe Krakowsky, was then Chairman and CEO of IPG Mediabrands. He recalls the period well.

Initiative was a traditional television-buying agency, and it was in the doldrums, not performing well. We knew that Mat would show up and shake things up. The place needed that kind of reinvention. There's a bit of a bulldozer quality to Mat, but at the same time, he does not seek out conflict. He says his piece and he comes to a conclusion about what he thinks the right course of action is.

At first, it felt to me as if Mat was frustrated because it dawned on him how daunting the task was at Initiative. He was worried that he was not making progress quickly enough. He was running a global company for the first time, and it was a really complicated organization. He could not do it all by himself. He mobilized his team, though, and six or eight months later, Initiative started to consistently win new clients.

I've observed that Mat has the ability to be self-reflective, which is interesting for someone who has the reputation of being a disrupter. When he first showed up at Initiative, his basic premise was, 'If you've been at Initiative for a while, you are on notice.' But despite this premise, he built an effective team, and he's definitely matured in his leadership style.

Baxter continued to overhaul the top management team, assembling a first-class group of executives, transforming the organizational structure and product lines, and revising the client development approach. Within a few years, Initiative went from #16 in the research firm RECMA's ratings[14] to #1 among media agencies. "And it was bloody hard," said Baxter, "but the team pulled it off. We won media agency of the year a number of times, which was extraordinary, given Initiative's history."

He noted that the US corporate culture was significantly more conservative and consensus-driven than the freewheeling Australian culture. He was learning that he could no longer be a sword-wielding troublemaker, attacking every problem in sight. "I learned that I had to mobilize my management team to do the hard work," he said, "and this required greater patience and empathy than I was used to. I figured out how to do this in the US, even though in many ways I missed the 'take no prisoners' days that I loved so much about Australia."

Tajer's 'entourage' eventually broke up, and Baxter was one of the last Australians to remain in New York. Tajer left IPG in 2017 and returned to Sydney for a job with Amazon in 2018. The other Australians went their various ways.

In early 2021, after Baxter had been at Initiative for five years, it no longer felt like a turnaround proposition, and he was getting itchy. He was proud of his team's accomplishments, and still got a buzz from pitching and winning new clients, but at age 43 he had energy and ambition to spare.

"IPG and I started talking about my next opportunity. Philippe knew that I loved a challenge, particularly if it involved a turnaround. I had expressed my desire to expand my world beyond media. So, he served up the CEO role at Huge and said, 'Here's your next turnaround. We want you take on the job and sort out Huge.' It was an enormously exciting opportunity, so I leaped at the chance to take it."

IPG CEO Krakowsky described the Baxter phenomenon:

Mat is a better hunter than anything else. He likes building new things that fit or meet a new set of needs. That's a really valuable skill set, given how much the marketing and media ecosystem is evolving. He's strategically really strong, and he likes pushing his vision fast, and moving people through change a little faster than they would prefer. After a few years, he's one of those people who gets restless and needs a new situation. So, in order to keep him at his most engaged and productive, every four or five years you have to figure out what his next challenge — and opportunity — will be.

Three months later, in 2021, IPG announced that Baxter would become Global CEO of Huge. It was to be his first role with a creative agency after two decades in media. What new challenges would this bring? He did not know. He suspected that a more creatively-driven business would add complexity to an established company culture. Creativity involves the emotions, he thought, and surmised that a creative agency might be more sensitive to things he might say. He thought that the agency people might need to be reassured that they're great, and brilliant, and talented, and that their new leader valued the notion of creativity. This was vastly different from working with media people, who are inherently more analytical, and transactionally inclined to 'just get on with it.'

He suspected that transforming Huge might require a lot of top-level support for the agency's creative culture, to make sure that everyone, from the creatives to the technologists, would feel comfortable with the changes he would lead.

"Huge might require a different kind of turnaround," he recalls thinking. "A very different one."

CHAPTER 4
INDUSTRY PRICING, REMUNERATION, AND SCOPES OF WORK

"Here's the scope of work ... and our profits."
Credit: Dennis Flad

Although Huge was an industry outlier at its founding — more like a technology provider than an ad agency — its clients were all major accounts who were spending serious amounts of money on typical advertising. They had existing relationships with many traditional ad agencies. Even though Huge was fundamentally different, it still swam in the same ocean as these other providers. But by being different in 1999, Huge was isolated from many entrenched industry practices, and as long as this continued, it would have a growth and profitability edge.

As time passed, though, and Huge began to diversify into traditional marketing, it came to be seen as just another agency, and it suffered accordingly. This certainly accounts for many of the growth and profit issues the company encountered after 2016.

When Baxter took the helm in 2021, one of his major challenges would be how to re-establish the company's uniqueness. Competitive singularity comes from being proactive, Baxter thought — delivering value that exceeds rather than simply meets client expectations. Being a good 'service provider' is not good enough.

In 1999, website development was a relatively new innovation, ready to be exploited for commercial purposes, and Huge was an early and creative innovator. The advertising mix that clients spent money on had been unchanged for decades: newspapers, television, magazines, radio and outdoor advertising. All of these channels would be dramatically affected by the growth and spend on the new disciplines: search advertising, social media, online video, and e-commerce.

The world's first web page went live on August 6, 1991. It was created by English computer scientist Tim Berners-Lee and dedicated to explaining the World Wide Web and its hyperlinks.[15]

THE FIRST WEBSITE, PUBLISHED IN 1991

World Wide Web

The WorldWideWeb (W3) is a wide-area hypermedia information retrieval initiative aiming to give universal access to a large universe of documents.

Everything there is online about W3 is linked directly or indirectly to this document, including an executive summary of the project, Mailing lists , Policy , November's W3 news , Frequently Asked Questions .

What's out there?
  Pointers to the world's online information, subjects , W3 servers, etc.
Help
  on the browser you are using
Software Products
  A list of W3 project components and their current state. (e.g. Line Mode ,X11 Viola , NeXTStep , Servers , Tools ,Mail robot , Library)
Technical
  Details of protocols, formats, program internals etc
Bibliography
  Paper documentation on W3 and references.
People
  A list of some people involved in the project.
History
  A summary of the history of the project.
How can I help ?
  If you would like to support the web..
Getting code
  Getting the code by anonymous FTP , etc.

A website was like an office building where commercial activities would take place, and expenditures to develop it were like construction costs. Once the building was up and operating, the various expenditures to get customers to come in the door and buy whatever was for sale were classified as marketing spend. These outlays were eventually tracked by industry data gatherers.

The expenditures tended to fall under broad categories — search advertising, social media, online video, and e-commerce — and might even include spending on website maintenance, site refreshes, and the addition of new site capabilities.

Huge entered the website construction business with its early clients, like IKEA and JetBlue, in 1999. Although founder David Skokna was a former ad agency executive, working originally at Deutsch, he was not part of the traditional Deutsch organization, which had a traditional creative reputation for TV, radio, print, outdoor, direct marketing, and promotional advertising. Instead, Skokna was in the new Deutsch Interactive Department, where he was an innovator and 'ideas guy.' After he resigned from Deutsch and convinced his childhood pal Sasha Kirovski to leave iXL Enterprises, where he was a software developer, the two formed Huge in 1999, marrying their capabilities to build websites that would push creative and technological boundaries, to create e-commerce opportunities for their clients.

They had the relative freedom to price Huge's services as they wished, creating project pricing for previously unseen sorts of website work. Their clients had no real ability to analyze or question the costs — each web development project was unique, like any blue-sky software development project. Although Skokna and Kirovski were hungry for new business, they still were able to price their services at a premium, reflecting the value of the work. Despite their high prices, Huge was much in demand, as their astonishing early growth rate testifies — the agency grew at an average of 31% per year for seven straight years.

By contrast, traditional ad agencies found themselves in less-than-desirable circumstances in 1999. They were still in the TV, radio, print and outdoor advertising business, but the industry's fee structure was rapidly changing, as the media-spend commission system was being abandoned in favor of labor-based fees. Under the media-spend system, if a client spent $10 million on media, an agency received a 15% commission on the spend, and that was the end of the story. How the agency carried out its mission — how many people it used, and how much they were paid — was of little concern to clients. By contrast, under the labor-based fee system, clients would pay for the costs of agency people assigned to their accounts, plus an additional amount to cover overhead, plus an agreed profit margin. This gave clients unheard-of levels of insight into internal agency operations and costs.

There were many reasons for a change in the agency compensation model. A key factor was the inflation in media costs for clients from 1975–2000, which saw media space and time inflate at twice the rate of GDP inflation, due to high demand and a shortage of media. Since agencies were paid on the basis of media spend, they benefited from media price inflation, collecting more revenue but incurring no additional costs. Yet, clients were paying the bill, not only for the increase in media spend, but also for increases in media remuneration based on the fixed-percentage commission. Clients were fed up with this situation and forced a change in the compensation model from media commissions to labor-based fees.

With this change, agencies were surprised to find that their clients, who had been marketing executives in the past but now included procurement and finance people, were terribly interested in the nuts and bolts of agency operations. "How much do you pay your employees?" they asked. "How much overhead do you incur to support your operation? What are the specific cost elements that make up your overhead? What kind of profit margin do you earn, and what should your profits rightfully be on our account?"

Unwisely, agencies let the Association of National Advertisers (ANA), the industry's trade group, define the structure of their labor-based fees rather than taking control and structuring a system for their benefit. The new standard labor-based fees had the same structure as government-contracting fees. If overall employee salaries plus benefits equaled $1 million, for example, these costs would be paid as 'direct costs.' If the agreed overhead rate was 100%, then there would be additional compensation of $1 million, identified as 'overhead costs.' Total costs would be $2 million. If the contract permitted the supplier to earn a 10% profit margin on the $2 million, the total fee would be $2.222 million ($2 million divided by 0.9). The 10% profit would be $0.222 million. Often, this formulation was shortened to 'the billing multiple is 2.222,' meaning that the employee salary cost of $1 million was multiplied by 2.222 to achieve fees of $2.222 million, at a 10% margin if the overhead rate was 100%.

Labor-based fees meant that clients could stick their noses inside the agency tent for the first time. Client procurement departments entered the picture and began to negotiate with agencies to lower their fees. Procurement professionals gained power as they developed an understanding of agency economics. They used various tools, like salary and overhead benchmarking, to compare one agency's costs to another's, and used this intelligence to drive down fees.

Agencies conceded to procurement-led fee demands. What else could they do if they wanted to retain their clients? There was always another agency, waiting in the wings, prepared to steal a major client by offering to do the work for less.

This was an awkward game for ad agencies to play, but since they still had some headcount fat left over from the salad days of media commissions, agencies could acquiesce to the demands for lower fees, cut their staffs, do the media or creative work and still generate a profit. The flaw in this thinking was that they agreed to a fixed number of people to carry out an unknown amount of work, since clients were not very explicit about how much an agency would have to do for a given fee.

One of the many things agencies did not anticipate was the relative loss of power in their client relationships. Giving in to clients and letting them determine how much would be paid, and how many people could be used, eroded agency power and influence. Where they had once dominated client relationships and provided proactive media and creative solutions, agencies now became more service-oriented as they scrambled to respond to ever-more-demanding clients. *Give them what they want* became the industry mantra, underpinning the client-service business model.

Simultaneously, after 2005, agency scopes of work expanded with the advent of digital and social deliverables, so workloads increased every year, even though client procurement teams were aggressively engaged in cutting fees.

Growing workloads and declining fees put pressure on agencies and encouraged them to become even more service-oriented and responsive, in order to retain their clients. Being proactive — debating tactics with clients, or even openly disagreeing with them about their strategic marketing programs — seemed commercially risky. Over a long period of time, agencies found themselves becoming more service-oriented and less proactive.

Baxter was dropped into Huge while it was struggling with growth. As a matter of principle and experience, he believed that slower growth was an outcome of the client service model. On the other hand, he was impressed with the organizational swagger he found at Huge, and convinced that the team had strengths that could be exploited if channeled in the right direction. He wanted to see the agency on a proactive trajectory, delivering exceptional value to clients and distinguishing itself competitively as a result. He wanted to see the company generating and implementing ideas that improved client results, something that could not happen under the client service model. He believed that improved client results would give Huge some pricing flexibility if he could wean it off of labor-based fees.

He committed to changing the client service model as a way of restoring Huge's growth and profitability.

How to do this was not at all obvious. He needed to enlist his management team in a sweeping transformation effort.

CHAPTER 5
THE HOLDING COMPANY OWNERS

Credit: Dennis Flad

Having the support of its owner — IPG, one of the big five global marketing communications holding companies — in its transformation was obviously necessary and critical for Huge.

What precisely are these holding companies? How do they operate, and how do they influence agency operations?

The big five are an internationally diverse group of players: the British WPP, with £12.8 billion in revenue in 2021; the American Omnicom Group, with $14.3 billion; the French Publicis Groupe, with €10.5 billion; the American IPG, with $9.1 billion; and the Japanese Dentsu Group Inc., with ¥5.2 trillion.

Baxter was put in charge of Huge by Philippe Krakowsky, IPG's new CEO, who took over the group in January 2021, replacing the retiring Michael Roth (2004–2020). Roth had overseen an increase in IPG's revenue from $6.4 billion in 2004 to $8.1 billion in 2020. Its stock price doubled from about $12 per share to $24 during Roth's 16-year tenure, but, as noted earlier, it had dipped to nearly $3 in 2008 before beginning a climb back upward.

Krakowsky was familiar with Huge's business performance history, having served as IPG's Chief Talent and Strategy Officer since 2002, before becoming COO in 2019. He appointed Baxter to engineer Huge's performance overhaul.

What would the balance be between Huge's transformation and its ability to deliver on its financial commitments to IPG? Who could know the answer in June 2021? Covid disruptions to revenue and costs were in play for IPG and its agencies, and for all of the holding companies and ad agencies worldwide. Uncertainty reigned. Clients were unsure about how much they should spend on media and creative services. Agencies were uncertain about their clients' plans for the present and the future.

HOLDING COMPANY FINANCIAL MANAGEMENT

IPG, like the other holding companies, lives and breathes *financial results*. Quarterly earnings are a very big deal. No holding company wants to risk failing to deliver the expected quarterly numbers to Wall Street.

At its simplest, holding companies are portfolios of various individually managed companies, and their measured performance is the sum of the outcomes of these individual companies. Holding company executives engage with each of the owned companies to assess their current financial performance and encourage them to make their assigned numbers. Only in this way will the holding companies themselves achieve their financial targets.

The financial plans for portfolio companies are in many cases 'stretch plans,' involving higher topline growth rates and wider margins than most agencies would like. There's nothing unusual about this. Financial management in any diversified corporation sees operating executives working feverishly to make their assigned targets. This is simply part of the corporate game. Any portfolio company falling short of planned performance needs to take early action steps, like safeguarding margins by cutting costs through downsizing, and achieving stretch revenue targets by taking on new business at prices or fees that may be less than ideal.

HOLDING COMPANY MARKETING INITIATIVES

Apart from carrying out their financial management responsibilities, holding companies seek to win big advertising clients by offering them 'holding company relationships,' which came into being during the digital/social marketing era, after 2005. The big-brand agencies within the holding company portfolios were then too narrowly focused on traditional advertising — they had not diversified their marketing capabilities to include digital and social media. The holding companies, which owned digital (and later, social) agencies, had the breadth within their portfolios to serve clients' diverse needs for advertising across all channels and disciplines.

In a holding company relationship, clients agree to largely, or exclusively, use the agencies owned by the holding company. In return for this exclusivity, and on the assumption that there are genuine economies of scale in holding company relationships, the holding companies could offer to do all of a client's media and creative work for competitive fees.

Often, these relationships involved holding companies offering to actually create bespoke agencies — new, stand-alone agencies dedicated to servicing a single account — for specific clients. One of the first was WPP's agency Enfatico, created for the personal computer and software maker Dell. It was announced with great fanfare in 2007 as "the greatest agency in the world," according to Casey Jones, Dell's Vice President of Global Marketing (and a former Grey executive). He declared that the two companies would develop a "nontraditional relationship... to achieve marketing objectives of Dell's that are simply not achievable either with our current roster of agencies or with a patchwork quilt of shops stitched together."[16]

The Enfatico initiative proved to be disruptive for all parties. Y&R, the core WPP agency for Enfatico, was robbed of resources to staff the new agency in Texas. The Dell marketing department had to reorient its agency activities in a very short period of time. Few of the hoped-for benefits were achieved, and Enfatico crashed and burned one year after its formation. WPP turned the Dell relationship over to Y&R, which had provided most of the agency leadership and resources for the bespoke agency.

Despite the failure of Enfatico, bespoke agency relationships have become quite the thing in advertising since 2007, with each holding company creating more of them than I can keep track of. Some ended up like Enfatico. In September 2021, health club franchiser Planet Fitness teamed with Publicis Groupe to create Team Lift, a bespoke agency that would handle "strategy, data and analytics, media planning and buying, creative and brand partnerships."[17] Less than a year later, Publicis and Team Lift were fired, and Planet Fitness returned to its original independent agency, Barkley, following the departure of the Planet Fitness CMO who'd initiated the bespoke agency relationship with Publicis Groupe.

Nevertheless, the trend continues. On August 10, 2022, the luxury automaker Bentley announced plans to change agencies "to help the brand evolve and transform its entire marketing communications strategy as it prepares for full electrification across its product range by 2030." What is Bentley's new agency? An IPG bespoke agency named iX. Headquartered in London, iX is a "purpose-built agency to service Bentley, and will draw on a range of resources from across IPG's portfolio."[18]

The holding company relationship movement means that holding companies have to organize marketing efforts at the corporate level, and be in a position to respond to holding company RFPs when they come over the transom from procurement, or through search consultants. I recently counted 79 corporate executives at one holding company who have customer responsibilities, as described in their LinkedIn profiles. Undoubtedly, these executives either promote, sell, or are otherwise involved in overseeing holding company relationships, in one form or another.

WPP AND PUBLICIS GROUP

Of the five big holding companies, two of them, WPP and Publicis, have taken holding company relationships so seriously that they've revised their corporate strategies, now positioning themselves as 'single corporate entities' rather than portfolios of individual companies.

Here are the August 2022 website descriptions of WPP and Publicis:

> **WPP.** "*We are the creative transformation company.* We use the power of creativity to build better futures for our people, planet, clients and communities. The 'new normal' is yet to be defined; creativity has the power to ensure that what comes next is better than what came before..."

By this formulation, and additional information on its site, WPP positions itself as a single global company with 109,000 people, operating in 110 countries. Its tab for 'WPP Companies' does not list a single WPP company, even though WPP is the holding company owner of integrated agencies like Wunderman Thompson, Ogilvy, VMLY&R, Hogarth, AKQA, Grey, GroupM, Mindshare, EssenceMediacom, Wavemaker, and mSix & Partners; public relations firms like BCW, Hill & Knowlton, Finsbury Glover Hering, and SVC; and specialist agencies like Superunion, Landor & Fitch, and CMI. This is just the tip of the iceberg — there are hundreds of companies owned by WPP.

Publicis goes further in describing itself as a single company in its website description:

> **Publicis Groupe.** "*Publicis Groupe has reinvented itself for the Connected Age by moving from Holding Company to a platform.* Highly modular, Publicis Groupe's Connecting Company model

is a unique platform that gives clients plug & play access to our best-in-class services. Supported by a Global Client Leader (GCL), our clients benefit from a borderless, seamless service that drives the alchemy of creativity and technology."

Publicis Groupe says that it is organized into four Solutions Hubs: Publicis Communications, Publicis Media, Publicis Sapient, and Publicis Health. The individual agency brands still exist and "share an operational backbone," with Epsilon, a data and tech company, "positioned at the center, fueling all the Groupe's operations with unparalleled data expertise." Finally, Publicis says, "We are able to deliver as the Power of One — driven by a common purpose, a powerful spirit, shared behaviors, great character and a relentless focus on our clients."

Publicis Groupe, like WPP, is a holding company that owns integrated agencies like Leo Burnett, Publicis Worldwide, Saatchi & Saatchi, BBH, Marcel, Fallon, MSL, and Prodigious. It owns digital and consulting operations like Publicis Sapient; media agencies like Digital, Spark Foundry, Performics, Starcom, and Zenith. And it owns healthcare agencies like Digital Health, Discovery USA, Heartbeat, Insync, Langland, Payer Sciences, Plowshare Group, and Publicis Health Media. Like WPP, Publicis manages its operations as independent profit centers. As with WPP, Publicis' major brands — Leo Burnett, Publicis Worldwide, Saatchi & Saatchi, and Zenith — receive very little airtime in the holding company's current communications. Today, communications focus only on 'the Power of One' — Publicis as a single company.

OMNICOM AND IPG

At the other end of the holding company spectrum are Omnicom and IPG, describing themselves as holding companies with portfolios of strong, creative, independent businesses. Their strength, each says in its own words, comes from the strength and independence of their individual companies. In practice, the CEOs of these individual companies run their operations as they see best. Baxter, as CEO of IPG's Huge, fits into this category.

Here is how Omnicom and IPG position themselves on their websites:

Omnicom. "Omnicom is an inter-connected global network of leading marketing communications companies. Our portfolio provides the best talent, creativity, technology and innovation to some of the world's most iconic and successful brands. We offer a diverse, comprehensive range of marketing solutions spanning brand advertising, customer relationship management (CRM), media planning and buying services, public relations and numerous specialty communications services to drive bottom-line results for our clients."

IPG. "Interpublic Group is a global provider of marketing solutions. With approximately 58,000 employees in all major world markets, our companies specialize in advertising, digital marketing, communications planning, media, public relations, and specialty marketing."

Omnicom and IPG stand in contrast to WPP and Publicis Groupe, focusing on the quality and independence of their individual agencies, rather than efforts of the corporate entity to provide 'center-led' creative, media, and other services to their clients.

A comparison of the recent share price performance of IPG, Omnicom (OMC), Publicis (PUB) and WPP is shown below. January 2021 share prices have been set at an index value of 100, and their 2022 and 2023 January share prices are compared to their 2021 prices. IPG and Omnicom lead their competitors Publicis Groupe and WPP in share price appreciation, at least for this recent period.

SHARE PRICE COMPARISON

January 2021 = 100

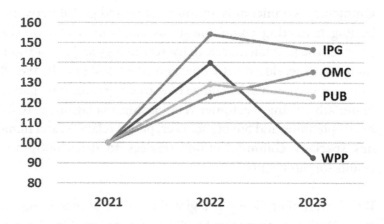

CEOs within Omnicom and IPG have to deliver their planned numbers, of course, as do all CEOs of holding company entities, but apart from this, they have the freedom to run their operations as they see fit. If this involves something as serious as engineering a strategic transformation, so be it — they have the freedom to transform themselves. Baxter, operating within the IPG framework, is empowered to carry out a transformation at Huge.

The turnaround of Huge's performance is an IPG *business priority*. The transformation of Huge is a *strategic initiative*, the strategy the agency is undertaking to achieve the required business turnaround. IPG did not ask Baxter to carry out a strategic initiative. It asked for a business turnaround.

———————

To begin the transformation in October 2021, Baxter assembled his leadership team for the first of three off-site management retreats that would take place during the coming 12 months. This first retreat focused on developing a revised mission for Huge, abandoning the client service model to become more proactive and effective for its clients.

CHAPTER 6
THE FIRST OFF-SITE MANAGEMENT RETREAT

OCTOBER 12–14, 2021

"This is an open discussion ... but keep your masks on!"
Credit: Dennis Flad

Covid was a major factor in the delayed scheduling of the first off-site ELT retreat, which would bring together 20 key executives for the first time since Baxter's June 2021 CEO appointment.

Those who planned to attend in person at the Weekapaug Inn on Block Island, Rhode Island, would have to provide proof of vaccination or a negative PCR test within 72 hours of arrival.

Others who could not travel, or didn't wish to attend in person, could participate via Zoom. Masks were required, and the windows and doors of the conference room would be kept open for ventilation during meetings. Executives were encouraged to dress warmly, as the cool sea breeze from the Atlantic would fill the conference room, coming in through the open French doors that looked out on Long Island Sound. Being chilly was a small price to pay; being together as a group was a positive development after more than a year of isolation and remote working.

In the run-up to the meeting, Baxter had met week after week, via Zoom, with small groups of Huge's 1,200 employees, who assembled by geographic location and were encouraged to raise issues of importance. Eventually, all employees were able to meet with him in this way. Baxter listened to feedback and did his best to respond, although it wasn't always easy for him to talk about the future of the agency and respond to comments that had a 'what's in it for me' subplot. He committed to transform Huge to secure sustainable growth and enhance employee career prospects, but the details of the transformation were not known — the planning effort was just beginning.

Understandably, these remote conversations were more symbolic than substantive. Employees had had a hard time as the pandemic ground on — family health issues, school complications, remote working, client instability, and high degrees of personal uncertainty complicated everyone's lives in the global company. Baxter was the fifth CEO in four years, but since many employees were young and had been with the company for only a short period, the CEO turnover did not loom large in their thoughts. They were willing to listen, and were pleased to see their new leader reach out and solicit their concerns. Nonetheless, there was a 'show me the money' dimension that was understandable. Employees who had worked for *Huge-as-it-is* could not help but wonder if they had a role in *Huge-as-it-will-be*, and what that might look like. They were looking for signs that would make them feel better about the future. This would be evident in every all-hands meeting for the next several months.

By contrast, the frequent CEO turnover was a major factor for the senior executives who assembled for the retreat in Rhode Island.

One of them whispered to me, "Mat has had a more positive effect in three months than the previous four CEOs did in four years." Expectations for the retreat ran high, but no one knew what was planned or how it would be conducted. The agenda was distributed at the last minute via email, and it did not give much insight into what was coming.

By the time of the leadership retreat, Huge had already engaged The Business Model Company (TBMC), a consulting firm based in London, which had just begun to audit the current client base and would help implement Huge's transformation in the latter months of 2021 and throughout 2022. The TBMC analyses were at a very early stage of development, though, and there was no useful output that could be used at the retreat.

Retreat participants included office presidents who were responsible for geographic regions centered in Brooklyn, Washington, Chicago, Toronto, Berkeley, London, Singapore, and Bogotá. In addition, there were corporate staff executives from Finance, Legal, HR, DE&I, Operations, Technology, Creative, and Customer Experience. It was an eclectic group, representing the most senior executives who had important managerial responsibilities. In the past, each of the execs had operated more-or-less independently — corporate decision-making was not a characteristic of the Huge culture. The offices operated as decentralized profit centers, and they worked independently of one another. The corporate staff executives in Finance, Legal, HR, and other functions worked with each of the offices on an ad hoc basis, solving whatever office problems arose.

The notion that a team of 20 executives would get together with the CEO to brainstorm the future of the company was an entirely new concept.

Furthermore, Baxter himself was an unknown quantity. Only his hard-working executive assistant, Tess Bricker, knew his operating style, having worked with him since 2018 at Initiative before moving to Huge with him. Since Bricker organized the logistics and prepared the agenda for the retreat, she knew what her boss was setting out to do. To the others, Baxter was young, energetic, and open, full of ideas, with a great track record from his media past, an Australian, willing to listen... but as yet an unknown quantity.

Baxter was in an imperfect situation. He certainly did not lack confidence in himself as an agency leader, but 100% of his past experience was with media agencies, not creative shops. He was expert in understanding media operations, and when confronted with a challenge at Initiative, IPG's media agency, he knew what to do: he could bring his extensive media expertise to bear and actively direct the efforts of his media executive team. He had done this successfully at Naked, at UM Australia, and at Initiative.

Huge was a different kettle of fish. Not only did Baxter not have personal experience with creative agencies, he didn't really know what kinds of detailed performance issues Huge had across its 12 offices. He had the financials for the first six months of 2021, of course, but those yielded few insights about operational considerations. What kind of work was going on for each of the clients? Was the work effective or not? Was it profitable or unprofitable? Were the clients likely to be short-term or long-term engagements? What were the particular strengths and weaknesses of each office, and the office executive teams? How strong was the financial foundation of the agency?

Since his appointment four months earlier, Baxter had dug deep to understand as much as he could about Huge's operations and expected results, but by the time he was ready to conduct this first executive retreat, he knew much less than he wanted to.

He was also unsure about what the meeting might accomplish. He did not expect a groundswell of new ideas about Huge's future. The ELT group was too large and too unused to working together to be productive in this way. He did not know the individual executives well enough at that early stage to sense who might contribute and who wasn't likely to. Consequently, he felt that the retreat might provide a forum where some thoughts about the future could be tested in real time — that is, if he could stimulate open, frank discussion. He knew that individuals tend to clam-up in group meetings, particularly in the presence of a new boss. One of the challenges would be to get people to open up and speak their truth.

In the absence of hard data, which were simply not available, he needed the ELT executives to anecdotally share their experiences at Huge over the years, and open up about what the agency had been, what it currently was, and what it could become in the future. The success of the transformation would depend on having a top leadership team that worked and thought in a uniform way about Huge's mission and modus operandi.

Baxter had a fixed idea about the future: he wanted Huge to be proactive and create positive results for clients as its mission. He believed that this mission would generate strong growth and give Huge the kind of pricing flexibility that agencies did not have in today's service model situation. Critically, he needed to find a way to steer the retreat's discussion in this direction.

He decided to use the first evening's dinner as an ice-breaker, and spend the following day and a half exploring seven fundamental questions:

1. What is the purpose of this get-together?

2. What makes a great company?

3. What sort of company do we want to be?

4. How do we set up the company for success?

5. What are the roles of the Chief Operating Officer and Chief Experience Officer?

6. What would 'great' look like at Huge?

7. What are our priorities for 2022?

He would lead the discussion by posing questions to the group and hoped that the answers, and dialogue that organically followed, would move things in the right direction.

The 20 executives sat next to each other, down one side of a long table. Baxter stood in front of the table, working without notes or slides. He would remain a standing presence, asking questions and stimulating discussion around the answers. Bricker, his assistant, and I kept detailed notes, and I recorded the discussions and would prepare transcripts for my later use. I did the same for the many executive interviews I conducted for this book — I recorded my interviews and prepared written transcripts.

The participants were dressed casually, as you might expect at an agency get-together, and Baxter wore a grey hooded sweatshirt, dark sweatpants, and fluorescent-orange trainers. He has a slight and sinewy build, and as he paced back and forth in front of this group, posing questions, pivoting, twisting, and probing, his moves were more than a little Jagger-like in front of his audience.

---

1. What is the Purpose of this Get-Together?

Baxter began the full-day Wednesday meeting by announcing, with a bemused look, that he was going to be the *Chief Antagonizer* for the next two days. "We're all adults," he said. "We have to be able to give and take without any hurt feelings. We've never been together before as a team. This is an important meeting. I want an open discussion, and this means that you must challenge what is being said, and so should I. If we hear something that we think is not right, we need to call it out. I do not want to be the only one who does this. We are in this together, and I will be your Chief Antagonizer, but I'd certainly like to see you step up as well.

"What is our strategy for making things happen? What is each person going to bring to the party? For my part, I'll expose you to the world of IPG, which is one of the many worlds we live in.

"One of the things I've learned about Huge in the past few months is that we are an organization marked by impatience and a desire for instant rewards and success. But some things take time and careful planning. An example is this transformation, which I think we'll still be working on by the end of 2022 and well into 2023, as we change how we work with clients.

"What makes a great company? Let's discuss great companies and the reason they're great. Let's go around the table. What makes a great company?"

Somewhat hesitantly, individuals volunteered the names of iconic companies: Amazon. Google. Apple. Netflix. Geico.

The group began to consider what greatness entailed. They offered up a list of descriptors. Growing. Outsmarting competitors. Thinking strategically. Taking risks. Investing for the future. Taking bold steps.

Baxter asked, "Do we have the right conditions to be a great company? Can you give me an example of a bold step we've ever taken?" There was dead silence.

He continued: "Lack of courage is due to lack of clarity. We think that we are brave, but our delivery is less than our belief that we are courageous."

From this point onward, the discussion followed a pattern. Baxter or one of the participants would pose a question. Others would volunteer short individual responses, one after another, with braver individuals stepping forward to advance the dialogue and teeing up new subjects to be debated. Baxter encouraged participation and received a greater number of responses. At a certain point, the group would pause and take in the sum of what was said. The responses gradually began to coalesce into a narrative on the nature of current industry practices, the way Huge operated, and ways it should operate in the future.

The discussion became a Socratic dialogue, kicked off by questions that led participants to provide opinions, points of view, arguments and answers. These eventually could be turned into a coherent story. The retreat reminded me of classroom discussions at Harvard Business School, where professors initiate case study method discussions by asking, "What is Mr. Jones' problem?" Students take over by staking out their positions and arguing with one another, with the professor retreating to the blackboard to document the progress of the discussion. Baxter asked his team what it takes to be great, but this segued into other subject areas: the nature of work, pricing, talent issues, how to sell, the nature of contracts, and other random and associated issues.

As time went on, the degree of participation increased, and executives began to listen to and to add to one another's comments.

A common expression emerged during the discussions. Someone would say, after hearing a particular comment, "Let me build on that…" or "My build is…" The remarks built on one another, like a PowerPoint presentation that adds successive bullet points, one by one, as the storyline evolved.

Things were soon moving so quickly that, even afterward, with my notes and the audio recording, it was impossible for me to disentangle the conversational pathways that led to the conclusions. Sometimes it was Baxter who drew the conclusions from the discussions. More frequently, that came from one or more of the participants, who reacted to aspects of the freewheeling discussion. In aggregate, the conclusions emerged from give-and-take kicked off by the early questions. I ended up with the list of questions and their summary conclusions, with an abundance of underlying background material.

The dialogue is summarized below. The fundamental questions are shown in bold. The conclusions are in *italic*. The discussions became richer and more animated as the retreat progressed. This material is a reflection of the conversational flow.

2. Q&A: What Makes a Great Company?

What makes a great company? *The list of great companies is a short one. Great companies are audacious, brave, true to their purpose, consistent, coherent, and fully aligned. We will need to embrace the qualities that define greatness. We already have a strong culture. We can mobilize this strength to achieve new goals. We have to avoid becoming risk averse, more worried about financial outcomes than doing the right thing for clients. We've had this problem in the past. We'll need to reorient ourselves.*

What are our attitudes about profits? *We have not been proud to make profits in the past. Profitability meant cutting corners, or doing quick work that was not our best. We over-invested with clients to generate great work, and the work often turned out to be unprofitable. We associated great work with unprofitability. Good work should create its own reward, and it should be highly profitable — we need to price it appropriately.*

Do we know 'what works' for the work we do for our clients? Do we know how to generate positive commercial results? *We have done all kinds of project work for clients, and some of it has been very effective, but not 100% of it. In the future, we need to be entirely consistent. Our work must exceed client expectations by delivering exceptional results. This will give us pricing flexibility for the future.*

Can we develop an organization that celebrates successes for ourselves and for IPG? *We need to educate our workforce about our new criteria for success. Toni Lowe [head of DE&I — Diversity, Equality and Inclusion — and formerly with the USAA financial services group] pointed out that USAA employees high-fived one another when quarterly profits were published. We could have this kind of pride-in-profits for ourselves and for IPG, but it will take some time and work.*

Do we have a culture of positive outcomes for clients? *Our culture may have accepted mixed outcomes in the past, but it needs to evolve so that 100% of outcomes are positive for clients. We have always done what clients expected of us, but clients have not always been as demanding as they should have been. We should always exceed their expectations. The work that we should be most proud of is that which works for our clients, driving improved results, even if this is not exactly what they are asking us to do. Work cannot be great if it does not contribute to their business success.*

Do we focus too much on how hard we work, rather than on what we achieve? *We need to be about outcomes, not about our activity. What we put into our work means little to our clients. How hard we work, how many types of research we do — who cares? We should only care about outcomes. Unfortunately, we often talk to clients about how much we put into our work, hoping to show them our serious commitment to our relationships. This is the wrong way to show commitment — doing consistently good work would be a much better way.*

What if we focus 100% on achieving results for clients? *It would be audacious. It would be right. But it would require big changes in the way we organize and think about things.*

Is there enough 'strategy' in the work we do? *If there are no strategic underpinnings in a proposed engagement with a new client, should we walk away? We would have to be relentless in this policy. We would have to be audacious and committed. We need to take our strategic work more seriously than we have in the past. We have certainly not explained to resistant clients that strategy is a core ingredient in delivering results. Doing fundamental strategic work ought to become a requirement for any new relationships.*

What does it mean to be bold? *Focusing on client results is bold, but for the leadership team, it is even bolder to figure out what it will take to get there! A results focus is clear and logical. The hard work will come with changing our culture, products, organization, and operational practices to get there.*

Do we have long-term relationships? *Our retention of project clients is lower than it needs to be. We would grow much faster if we could increase our client retention rates. We probably need to focus more on retention rather than on pursuing new clients. The most successful engagements are surely our longer-term ones. This means that we have to be more proactive in selling in future work with clients, rather than being satisfied when we have completed projects.*

Is being results-focused enough of a differentiator to distinguish us from the consulting firms? Is there a space we can occupy where we are neither an agency nor a consulting firm? *We could focus on helping CMOs become more respected and successful within their organizations. Currently, they are turning over and moving on every two to three years, and agency relationships are then up for grabs when a new marketing leader comes in. In theory, we could help CMOs break this cycle, but we'd have to train our Client Executives to be more effective in this respect.*

3. Q&A: What Sort of Company Do We Want to Be?

What sort of company do we really want to be? Should we continue to call ourselves 'an agency?' *There's a gap between consultants and agencies. We could be called problem definers, creative and technological problem solvers, strategists, or strategic partners. But we don't really fit as consultants or as ad agencies, particularly if we cease to do integrated marketing. We need to create a new category.*

What is the greatest benefit a client can have working with Huge? What about in the future? What is the highest-order benefit? *If a client said, 'Huge helped me understand our marketing performance problems, and then helped me solve them,' this would be the greatest testimonial we could hope for.*

Isn't low growth the major client problem? *Clients never discuss their growth problems with us, but growth is what keeps them awake at night. They are afraid to discuss their problems, as if this makes them appear weak when they want to appear strong. It would take a genuine sense of partnerships to create this kind of intimacy, and we do not always have these kinds of partnerships. If we are vendors, they will never ask us to help them grow. So even if growth is a major problem, we will be unable to discuss it or work with them on it unless we are seen as legitimate, trusted partners.*

Shouldn't we want to work with brands that want to realize their full growth potential? *Yes, but first we have to be seen as partners. Some clients do not have growth today, so we may first need to know how create growth where none exists. It makes sense for us to be identified as 'growth partners' who are obsessed with achieving client growth. Our employees will love this — it will be motivating and is entirely consistent with the kind of company they feel they are working in.*

Can we become a company that accelerates growth? *This is what venture capital and private equity firms do. We could do the same thing, but do it with technology and creativity rather than through financial engineering. We could become a firm that is seen to produce* 'creative capital.' We could be seen to be a performance accelerator that uses creative capital to create a ROI for clients. That's not completely far-fetched. Our clients should expect to have a positive return on their investment in creative capital.

4. Q&A: How Do We Set Up the Company for Success?

How should our crafts work with one another? *The office presidents have been the key players. The other crafts[19] operate in a more subordinate way in each office. Our client executives manage the interface between clients and crafts. We need to develop a clear vision for what each craft should do, and how they could deliver more value, working collaboratively with and relating to the client executives who run our accounts. Today, it's more hierarchical than collaborative. We need to move to a more collaborative structure, where each craft makes more notable contributions to client success.*

Do employees work for offices or for Huge? *Offices have been the focus in the past, but shouldn't we see our employees as working for Huge, not for their crafts or for their Office Presidents? Past hiring was geographically based. But if we handle this on a more global basis, hires could be 'for Huge, by craft.' We would need to change the way we recruit and hire. We should simplify our job titles, too, because they vary by office, and we now have more than a hundred job titles.*

What does the executive team need to do to be more familiar with the work we do around the world? *Right now, we know very little. The work goes on in the offices, and it is not transparent to anyone at the center. The only way to know what work we are doing is if there are regular top-level reviews of our client work. This is something we have not done.*

What would these reviews entail? *These reviews would need to include: 1) what work we are doing for each client; 2) if that is the right work to improve client results; 3) whether we have the right number of people on the account, along with the right talent for the client's problems; 4) if we have the right relationship and fees, and are respected as a business partner; 5) what future projects should follow* *the conclusion of the existing work; and 6) whether this work is collaboratively planned with and understood by clients.*

How often should these reviews take place? *This process needs to take place quarterly, led by the CEO and members of the ELT. Our client executives will need to be accountable for the work they are doing and why the work is being carried out. This is not the case today. We need a uniform way to describe our work so that all clients can be viewed in a uniform way, no matter what office is involved.*

5. Q&A: What are the Roles of the CXO and the COO?

Lisa De Bonis (Soon-to-be Global Chief Product Officer): *The CXO should represent 'why' and the COO should represent 'how.' The CXO should unite with strategy as a craft to help with the evolution from 'what we make' to 'why we make it,' and figure out how to measure it, along with ensuring that data-driven strategic work is at our core.*

Mark Manning (Global COO): *The COO should figure out how to get it done. This will involve implementing the TBMC change program, troubleshooting our challenges, and keeping abreast of client progress via TRR surveys and other means. We definitely need to develop a more uniform client management approach — currently, every client executive runs things in a unique way. The TBMC program is in the 'calm before the storm' period because data are being gathered and processed. It will deliver insightful, actionable feedback. The transformation will include: 1) what client archetypes we need to create; 2) how these clients will 'come in' to Huge, as projects, as relationships, and to solve defined problems; 3) what capabilities we need to develop; 4) what products and services we need to develop; 5) how we prepare for pilot projects with clients; 6) what kinds of commercial models we must develop for our client relationships.*

6. Q&A: What Does 'Great' Look Like?

What are our thoughts about strategy? *Strategy is current underpurchased by our clients. This is probably because we undersell it! We have to walk away from potential client relationships if strategy* cannot be at the core of what we do together. We should not do work that does not have strategic relevance, so we need to ensure that we have strategy at the core of each of our new relationships.

What are our thoughts about pricing? *Pricing is a high-level problem that we must solve. Labor-based pricing is based on the wrong concept — we're paid for our costs, rather than for our outcomes or the success of our accomplishments. We need to develop and implement a pricing strategy that sees us charging appropriate prices for the work we do, not for our internal costs, even though client procurement departments expect to pay us on the basis of labor-based costs. We have to establish a new pricing approach and have our new clients accept it as the basis of our remuneration.*

What are our thoughts about scopes of work? *We need to develop SOWs proactively, rather than wait for clients to tell us what they want us to do. Being more proactive is something we will need to build into our culture if we are to focus on helping clients solve problems and generate results.*

What else is involved in being proactive? *Tracking what we do. We need a new approach for timesheets, project management systems and SOW documentation. All these need to be uniform across all geographies, offices and clients. They need to be rigorous and useful in order for leadership to know what work is ongoing and whether or not it is the right work for clients.*

Where do we stand with DE&I?

Toni Lowe: *We need to develop an anti-racist culture. This needs to be built into the culture of Huge. It is a bigger challenge than simply having affinity groups or other initiatives. DE&I must permeate our organization. We need to be welcoming and provide a true sense of belonging for all our employees, not just our diverse employees. DE&I represents a complete culture reorientation. We need to establish DE&I-related key performance indicators (KPIs) for each member of the executive team.*

7. Baxter Summary: What are our Priorities for 2022?

We need to significantly increase our sales over the next three years — through the end of 2024. This must be an outcome of our transformation.

At what margin? We can have better control over margins if we develop a new pricing approach.

Improved margins can only come about through our transformation and changing our pricing approach.

Let's not forget, though, that the transformation will divert the efforts of the leadership team. Transformation is both the means to move forward and a constraint on our efforts, two sides of the sword. We have a business to run and a new business to create. We have to do both in the coming years.

We must grow, unify our act on a global basis and become more mature as an organization. We need to convert ourselves from a 'light bulb' for our clients and become, instead, a 'laser' whose efforts drive improved results for them.

How do we train/communicate with our people? Our folks need to have a coherent understanding of our strategy, from top to bottom. Every Huge employee needs to understand our purpose and our approach. Each employee needs to be an ambassador for results-driven work. This will require a major communications and cultural-development effort.

Our people need to be led, not just by office management, but by the executive team. Leadership is our collective responsibility. Understandably, our employees will want to know what's in it for them, and if we put forward a transformation that is credible and logical, everyone will benefit. The work will be more satisfactory. We will be in a better position to pay people what they are worth, and for what they contribute. What we face now is the challenge of designing our success, not only for our clients and IPG, but for our employees as well.

We're going to transform Huge because it is strategically desirable. We will lead this transformation as a management team.

CHAPTER 7
THE BUSINESS MODEL
COMPANY LIMITED

"Forty-five products! No more ... no less!"
Credit: Dennis Flad

The October 2021 leadership retreat prepared the soil for Huge's transformation, and it met Baxter's expectations. A list of 22 actions were identified, but these actions were more symbolic than concrete — they did not themselves provide a foundation for the transformation. The results were conceptual, involving the *idea* of the transformation, and the most important outcome was agreement on a changed mission for Huge's work with clients.

In the future, the company[20] would dedicate itself to improving client results. Specifically, this meant improved client growth rates. Huge would focus on becoming a *growth acceleration company* for its clients.

The implications of the mission change were far-reaching, and every member of the ELT had private thoughts about what this meant for the company and for themselves. Jason Musante, the veteran Chief Creative Officer, reflected on his five-year effort to rebuild the Creative Department during Huge's low-growth period. This included initiating and carrying out 'integrated marketing' for clients, particularly in the Brooklyn office. Although he understood and agreed with the logic of the mission change, he decided to move on and leave the creative management challenge to new leadership. He left following the retreat, and Baxter named Fura Johannesdottir, the company's London-based Chief Design Officer, the new Global Creative Officer. She had joined Huge 18 months earlier, from Publicis Sapient London. Johannesdottir attended the retreat via Zoom, and she was ready to take on the challenge of repositioning design and creativity for Huge's new, client-centric mission.

The other members of the ELT remained on the job and buckled up for an interesting ride into the future. Baxter won their support with logic and energy, as he actively led the discussions about what it takes to be successful with clients, and the reality of Huge's current practice and culture. Importantly, he motivated the executives to share honest assessments of Huge's past and current capabilities, and to see their need to work together to create a new future. The call for change led to the creation of a tighter group that pledged to work together on the challenge.

Baxter enjoyed his self-styled role as Chief Antagonizer. He did not force any personal ideas on the team. He used the executives' own assessments of Huge in getting them to acknowledge the need to revise the company's mission and operations.

The retreat was a conceptual win for the ELT. Yet, much more would be required to turn this notion of transformation into a fundamentally changed company. Huge needed a vigorous drive that fully engaged each member on individual projects that supported the collective change program. Their respective efforts, specialized as they were by discipline, had to fit together like pieces of a puzzle. Their work had to be coherent within their specialties, and capable of being integrated into the broader change program.

Like the rowers in an eight-person shell, the company's executives had to work individually and in unison. The boat had to move forward, not only to advance the transformation cause but also to continue to service existing clients and deliver appropriate financial results while the transformation was taking place.

From his earliest days at Huge, Baxter had felt that the global center had to become more unified and coherent. He believed that it would be impossible to effect a transformation with a company made up of a dozen offices operating as distinct mini-agencies. The discussions at the retreat confirmed his instinct — not a single member of ELT suggested that Huge should carry out 12 office transformations. They seemed to understand the idea that they had to create a single global organization, with a single-minded culture and purpose. Encouraged by this, Baxter concluded that the 12 offices could be wound-up as profit centers, but he kept this to himself and decided to confront the matter another day. Some offices would close, while others would be transformed into 'experience centers,' designed and equipped for post-Covid ways of working.

But before he could discuss and begin this change, which he knew would be dramatic, Baxter had to figure out how to deal with three more urgent priorities: 1) how to create a single Huge culture that put the client, rather than the office, front and center; 2) how to develop products, rather than services, that would solve client growth problems; and 3) how to reorganize the company's management of resources so it could operate on a single, global basis, allocating executives to clients from a single pool of resources. Yet, these three priorities did not cover all of his concerns. He knew, for example, that a new sales approach would have to be developed and used for the training of Client Partners. This could have to come later, though, along with a pricing strategy for the company's new products.

In the near term, he needed to create momentum for the initiatives he wanted to lead. For this, he enlisted TBMC, the consulting firm he had met serendipitously and hired in September 2021.

TBMC provided a clear framework for business model transformations within the creative industry. It was not the kind of firm that said, 'We can help you figure out the future,' and then did some analyses to identify what this new future would be. Instead, TBMC had a very precise view about what their clients needed. They were dogmatic about sustainable business model change. Their approach was: 'Follow our program, and you will be successful. We know what you need. We know how to get you there.' The way they described their practice dovetailed with what Baxter was looking for, and he hired TBMC immediately after hearing their approach and checking their references. He had had no previous experience with them. Fate brought them together at a time when TBMC was the partner Baxter needed to accelerate Huge's transformation.

TBMC is a London-based management consulting firm that was originally on a short-list of consultants being considered by Mark Manning, who was to become COO, for his work with a global client. The client was being jointly handled by a number of Huge offices around the world, and coordination of the various efforts was complicated. The client wanted Huge to move with greater velocity, and Manning knew the agency couldn't do this by operating in such a fragmented way. "We needed one global chess board for this client," he said, "and we needed an experienced consultant to help us implement the necessary changes." He prepared a consulting brief in mid-July 2021 and went out shopping for an appropriate firm.

Caroline Johnson, a co-founder of TBMC in 2016, was one of the recipients of Manning's brief, and the two of them had a telephone conversation in July of 2021. Manning defined his need as "the development of a future-fit operating system" for the global client.

Johnson listened sympathetically to Manning's description of the complications associated with managing the global client, and they explored the kinds of changes that would be required. Johnson understood what was needed, and it was clear that she had the expertise to help, but TBMC did not work in a narrow way on single-client issues. "We don't really work this way," she told Manning, "but if you're willing to have another conversation with us — it will take an hour or so — I would like to tell you what we do more broadly. We work to revise the business model of entire agencies, and if we work together, you will get what you're looking for with this client... and a whole lot more."

This conversation took place shortly after Baxter had joined Huge. He was thinking about appointing Manning as COO after the two had discussed at length what was broken and needed to be fixed. Manning, who was thinking about Huge's big-picture needs, agreed to schedule a second call with TBMC to hear their pitch.

In their follow-up conversation, Manning listened to Johnson's description of TBMC's business model transformation practice, was impressed with what he heard, and arranged for TBMC to present to Baxter and members of the ELT. This presentation took place in mid-August 2021.

The consultancy discussed its business model practice and provided Huge with three references. "I was absolutely blown away by what I heard," Baxter told me many months later. "I had my own vision of what Huge needed: a new mission that focused on generating performance improvements for clients, a shift from service to product for what we offered, and a single global organization for our operations. TBMC spontaneously presented their concepts, and I knew in a minute that we were 100% aligned. It was either a lucky accident, or we were fated, somehow, to work together. I did not waste time wondering how this happened. I wanted to hire them on the spot."

The references checked out, and TBMC was given the green light to prepare a program plan and budget. After some discussion and fine-tuning, the 2022–2023 TBMC–Huge plan was approved on September 15, 2021.

TBMC's work got under way on September 28, 2021. Like many consulting programs, it began as a quiet data collection exercise that examined Huge's operations for the previous five years, from 2016 through 2021. For instance: What was the company's situation in the recent past, and how has it changed? Who were and are Huge's clients? What kind of work has been carried out for each of them? What is the history of Huge's fees, headcounts, and fees by client?

What were the profit margins? What does the overall profile of clients look like today, by size and type of relationship? What do the most successful clients look like? What about the least successful?

Johnson and TBMC's Sara Fielding, both in London, worked with Patrick Burke, Huge's Director of Finance, to identify the data that would be needed. The consultants did not do any of the actual data-gathering work; they worked with Huge executives to define the data needs, and the execs pulled the information together themselves. "It's important for our clients to do the hard work from the beginning," Johnson told me. "This is their transformation, not ours, and the only way to get buy-in for a business model change is to get client executives engaged early and throughout the process."

Once the data were pulled together, they told a coherent story about Huge's client operations, and this story would align precisely with the qualitative conclusions that came out of the leadership retreat. A few top clients accounted for an overwhelming percentage of Huge's profits; others were much less profitable. New clients, engaged over the previous four years, were expensive to develop, and client development costs were not always fully covered by ongoing operations. Huge offered hundreds of different service offerings to its portfolio of clients in pursuit of the client service business model.

In short, the agency's current way of doing business was suboptimal, even when great work was being done for clients, and it didn't provide a basis for sustainable success and growth. The offices, which were responsible for client development activities and the ongoing management of a large customer base, were adding less value than needed. A different business model was required. Huge could aspire to operate with no more than 50 top clients, developed and run on a globalized basis. It did not need a network of independent profit-center offices to engage in client development activities.

Johnson presented her business case for a complete model change to the ELT on November 16, 2021, exactly one month after the retreat. These findings were just a warm-up for the sweeping transformation program. Like the retreat, the business case set the stage. The real work would begin when the 'what do we do about it' phase would commence, with each of the Huge executives fully engaged in creating a new, globalized, client-centric future.

TBMC had its genesis in 1992, when Johnson, who had been an account executive in London with Grey Worldwide, left the agency and joined forces with Zoe Day, formerly of Howell Henry, to create a consulting firm that helped to improve agency operations after an agency was acquired by a holding company. The Johnson Day Partnership, as it was called, conducted post-acquisition due diligence analyses, prepared performance-improvement plans, and presented the business cases to acquirers. They surfaced many considerations. What should the acquirer do with the acquired business? What were the performance-improvement priorities? How would these priorities be carried out? Should the acquirer preserve the agency as an autonomous profit center, or should it be rolled into another entity?

The consulting business flourished, particularly through work with WPP, because WPP was then, early in its life, acquiring a number of below-the-line agencies. Johnson Day developed a set of tools and diagnostics that standardized their data collection and analytical methodologies. Their work allowed them to say, "This is what you need to do with this business, and what will happen if you succeed. On the other hand, if you do not make these changes, the current trajectory of the business will be much less attractive — and here is what it will look like."

Johnson Day worked closely with Results International, the London-based M&A advisory firm that helped acquirers buy agencies, and helped agencies prepare themselves to be sold. Results International purchased Johnson Day in 2010 and integrated the consultants into its M&A practice. Johnson became a Results International Partner, working over the next decade on M&A, investment strategies and management buyouts. She specialized in developing business model change programs for strong independent agencies — those at the point of wanting to get their businesses ready to attract suitors who'd pay top dollar if they had top-line revenue growth and sustainable EBITDA, performing well ahead of the sector.

After a decade with Results International, Johnson wanted to work independently as a business model change consultant. She didn't wish to continue doing the financial advisory work that was a big part of Results International's practice. She left amicably and set up a new firm, the Clear Transformation Company, with Sara Fielding, her colleague from Results.

Clear Transformation consulted with the digital design and communications agency AKQA from 2010 to 2012, helping Ajaz Ahmed, its founder, sell the business to WPP. Johnson and Fielding then worked with LBi, the digital creative agency that was sold to Digitas in 2013. Subsequently, they helped The Engine Group sell itself to Lake Capital, and Lake Capital became a client for a number of business model engagements. Johnson and Fielding consulted for Karmarama before it was sold to Accenture in 2016.

In 2017, when Johnson was looking for a partner to help expand her consulting operations, she met Rob Connolly, CEO of 360i, a London digital creative agency owned by Dentsu. After discovering a wide range of common interests, they joined forces and co-founded The Business Model Company.

Later in 2017, TBMC invited Tim Williams of the US-based Ignition Consulting Group to join as a business partner. Johnson and Williams had a long-standing relationship, and a shared vision about pricing and revenue models, and they had collaborated on a number of client assignments. Williams continues to run Ignition, as well as operate as a partner on various TBMC programs.

TBMC works in-depth with only a few clients at a time. It is a small organization — Johnson, Connolly, and Williams are the firm's leaders and consultants. They leverage their capabilities to carry out large transformation programs by having a standardized approach and template-based methodologies for their practice. TBMC establishes the framework, provides the schedule and animates clients' executive teams, who end up doing the work under TBMC's direction. Getting clients to the point of full involvement is one of their major capabilities.

TBMC'S CONCEPT

Johnson is an articulate, forceful presenter who leaves you with little doubt that TBMC has a clear view about its business and expects to deliver 100% success for its clients if they follow the consultancy's approach. "We design and implement new models through very fast change programs, usually lasting between nine and 12 months," she told me. "Client involvement in the program is what creates the necessary commitment." She described her beliefs and experience:

- TBMC's clients scale their operations through a re-engineering of their business models. Agencies today do not run themselves to achieve scale — each client is run as a separate service business, and each client's services are different from other client's services. The current agency business model is fragmented; there is no way a CEO or top management team can improve agency performance. The service model is a dead end for them.

- Agencies provide services when what their clients really need are products that are tailored to solve problems. You cannot scale a service-oriented business. You can certainly scale a product-oriented business. The world is moving to productization, and TBMC helps clients move to that model. It is a key concept for the consultancy's programs. Clients transform themselves from service-oriented companies into product-oriented companies. This is the secret to achieving scale and improving agency financial performance.

The shift from service orientation to product orientation is an essential change required by the TBMC playbook. The firm leads its agency clients to develop standard products that are sold by agencies to their clients. The products are designed to meet their customers' needs for performance improvements. Selling products at a price releases agencies from the labor-based practice of negotiating man-hour costs, team sizes, and the number of weeks or months needed for an assignment. There is no discussion about hours expended or how much overhead the agency incurs. The product is the product; the product is what the agency sells; the product has a price; the product solves performance problems. The shift from service-orientation to product-orientation is the way agencies can reassert their value-added and provide their expertise, something that the service model does not permit.

This is all well and good, and a productization approach makes strategic and economic sense, but an agency that currently generates all of its revenue from allocating employees to service-oriented client work is in an awkward situation. How does it transform itself into a product-led organization when it has no experience with products, has no products to sell, and is 100% organized to provide services?

TBMC acknowledges that each of its clients has to run, simultaneously, on two tracks: the business-as-usual track that generates revenue and profits, and the transformation track that puts the new ways of working in place. The firm is involved only in organizing the transformation track. It is up to the client's top management, and particularly the CEO, to manage the business-as-usual track while the parallel transformation work is being carried out.

This two-track challenge was a major activity for Baxter, who had to keep one eye on Huge's current clients and financial performance and the other on the progress of the transformation. He had to keep the business running, but at the same time, he had to signal to the organization that important changes were coming. He had to offer the prospect of a brighter future for Huge without killing the momentum of the current business.

Baxter faced this problem every month when he spoke to employees at all-hands meetings. He didn't use these occasions to introduce TBMC or outline the nature of the consultants' program. TBMC worked behind the scenes with the leadership team on the various aspects of the transformation program; the mechanics were not visible to the rank and file organization. The average employee, working in one of the company's 12 offices, had no idea that TBMC existed and was helping to shape the future of the company.

Within the ELT, the transformation program was codenamed Project Polpo — *polpo* being the Italian word for octopus, the complicated sea creature with eight arms, a soft and adaptable body for squeezing in and out of tight spaces, and a high brain-to-body weight ratio. Baxter laughed when I asked him how the project name came about. "It's obvious, isn't it? An octopus is not very elegant in appearance, but when it goes into action, it's amazing. Did you know that the eight arms have intelligence capabilities that are independent of the central brain? That's exactly what we need for this transformation!"

Manning, the recently appointed COO, was put in charge of Polpo. Johnson worked directly for him, but the intellectual underpinnings of the initiative — the project plan, milestones and outputs — were straight out of the TBMC playbook.

TBMC LANGUAGE AND VOCABULARY

TBMC uses a unique, stylized vocabulary when describing advertising industry practices and the content of the consultancy's transformation program. Over time, I began to hear Huge executives using TBMC terminology when describing what they were doing and where it was heading. This was a sure sign that the consultants were having a cultural impact on the ELT's thinking. Some examples of TBMC's language and concepts are described below.

1. **Goodwill Service Model.** All companies have business models that define their professional business philosophies and practices. Some of these models are good but most are not. Agencies typically follow the Goodwill Service Model, which is based on delivering and over-delivering services, hoping that a bucket of goodwill will be created that encourages clients to reward the agency disproportionately. That never actually happens. Agencies end up providing the same services as every other agency, leading clients to see them as commoditized suppliers who lack differentiation from one another. The talent and the investment agencies make in the Goodwill Service Model is wasted — agency talent becomes marginalized in this commodity business. Creativity is a service, not a sustainable differentiator. As such, this model is an economic dead-end and needs to be abandoned.

2. **Circles and Squares.** Agencies provide services (circles) to clients, but they soon realize that these circles are not generating enough value. So, they create or buy-in products (squares), like technology, data/analytics, strategy/insights, etc. Where this fails is that circles and squares do not mix well in an agency offer. If an agency begins to productize or repackage higher-value products, it is difficult to provide these as part of a service offer — to sell squares to clients as part of a circle offer. The products have to go through the circle system to be monetized. Monetization fails; products are paid for as low-value services. Instead of mixing

circles and squares, agencies need to change the whole system. Squares need to be offered and sold separately to clients, and circles need to be wound down entirely. A new business model based on productization needs to replace the legacy service business model. Squares need to replace circles. The business transformation involves the replacement of circles by squares.

3. **Client Archetypes and Value Journeys.** Most creative businesses do not have viable revenue models. This is one of the main reasons they find it difficult to scale and make money. Mastering the right revenue model is fundamentally important to the sustainability and scalability of a business. Employing the wrong model contributes to client churn and talent burnout. For most creative shops, new business is a zero-sum game, but is always celebrated internally — much more than organic client development.

4. **Front Doors.** Agencies need to think about how clients engage with them — how clients 'enter' their businesses, how they 'arrive,' and what their expectations are. Agencies need to establish new front doors to greet their clients and provide entry to the agency's capabilities. What does this mean? Historically, the way the clients arrive at agencies is via a single doorway that has two doorbells, one for projects and one for briefs. This single entryway, known as 'the brand communications doorway,' has not changed over the last 20 years. It may have been the right entry point for clients decades ago, but over time, agencies have invested heavily in consulting, innovation, technology, and data/analytics. Yet, clients still come in through the very narrow brand communications doorway. This needs to be changed. Instead of the single doorway with two doorbells — projects and briefs — agencies need three doorways that have different names. Every agency needs to create three unique front doors that reflect the client archetype language and are the main gateways into the business for clients. These front doors need to be defined from the top down (highest level of value that you can deliver to your clients) not from the bottom up (services you wish to sell).

5. **Drawers.** Clients who enter one of the three front doors of an agency will have access to a product portfolio that allows them to view and engage with full product suites from the start. Within these portfolios are 'drawers' that contain particular products for each front door. For example, if a client enters an 'experience transformation' door, it will be able to access all the drawers that contain products designed to solve experience transformation problems. For each drawer, there are unique, high-level, client-facing documents called the promise and delivery statements. These statements create a new language that captures exactly what the client can expect, from product output to high-level outcome. Agencies that are transforming themselves to become productized need to develop product portfolios with drawers containing products, each of them with unique promise and delivery statements.

Once Project Polpo was officially launched after the October retreat, and TBMC completed and shared its diagnoses of Huge's existing business and clients, the transformation program came to life. ELT members, working collectively with Manning and Lisa De Bonis — who joined Huge from Accenture Interactive in London — developed a view of the company's client archetypes, front doors, product offers, value journeys, and promise and delivery statements. The work proceeded, and the ELT presented its progress from time to time, using TBMC terminology that was increasingly becoming Huge's vocabulary.

ELT meetings, which took place via Zoom every two weeks, covered Huge's progress on each of these fronts. Non-ELT members associated with various parts of Polpo were invited from time to time, and they, too, presented progress plans and used the TBMC vocabulary. Anyone who attended and was not familiar with the TBMC vocabulary would have been completely lost.

Here is an unedited snippet of a Polpo Playbook Review that took place by Zoom on February 8, 2022. The discussion was led by De Bonis, who'd been promoted to Chief Product Officer, a key position in the newly productized Huge. Here, she was explaining the framework she'd use to review Polpo's progress:

Before jumping into the value journey for each archetype in each door, let us understand the intent behind the framework and each part of the structure. The front door, as we said, is the reason the client engages with us. Client archetype is a summary of the high level goal the client is looking to achieve. The client buyer is a C-suite level client we are contracting and partnering with to deliver outcomes. The commercial value journey is the key concept framing how we will deliver value for the client in the context of that door. Output delivered is the high-level strategy they are planning to follow, to deliver the outcomes, and achieve their goal. And the commercial outcome is the business level KPI linked to the goal, objective, and strategy.

This was a meaningful dialogue, not just buzzword gibberish — every carefully parsed word had substance and meaning to the transformation players. Furthermore, and perhaps most importantly, the leadership team's adoption of TBMC's vocabulary was a clear sign that Huge executives were running the show, and bringing about the transformation. This was not a cookie-cutter initiative run by generalist management consultants, which is all too common when outside advisers are brought in to effect change in an organization.

Johnson developed the TBMC vocabulary with this purpose in mind. I asked her about vocabulary in one of our early interviews, and she made it clear that language was one of the explicit tools that help to bring about change and success. Here's how she put it:

I do not believe that you can create cultural change and transformation if you do not completely change a client's language and give them something different that is visual and repeatable. Clients do not realize that it is happening at the beginning, but once you get them talking about 'front doors,' for example, that ticks so many different psychological boxes that you capture their hearts and minds, and you get them to start repeating this new language, which spreads out across the organization. For me, this is the most important and powerful thing that we do.

In her 2021 book, *Cultish: The Language of Fanaticism*, linguist Amanda Montell showed through numerous examples how sect leaders use cult-like language to create cohesion and exert control over their members. However, she tempered her critical analysis with the recognition that "the motives behind culty-sounding language are not always crooked. Sometimes they are quite healthy, like to boost solidarity or to rally people around a humanitarian mission." She explained:

> *Language is a leader's charisma. It is what empowers leaders to create a mini universe — a system of values and truths — and then compel their followers to heed its rules. Words are the medium through which belief systems are manufactured, nurtured, and reinforced. Language is a way to get members of a community on the same ideological page. To help them feel like they belong to something big.*[21]

By April 2022, Baxter's leadership team had settled on the concept and names of Huge's three front doors. They were: 1) Experience Transformation; 2) Technology Realization; and 3) Growth Creation. Once a potential client entered through one of these doors, it could experience five possible 'value journeys,' represented by drawers containing three specific products each. Since each front door had five drawers, and there were three products per drawer, each front door opens onto 15 products. In aggregate, the company's three front doors would have 45 offerings. And so, Huge needed to develop 45 new products across the three front doors, each with a name and a unique promise and delivery statement.

Soon, work was afoot to develop the products and the pricing formula for each of them.

One month later, in May 2022, a trade press article announced that Huge would be swapping many of its physical offices for experience centers and co-working spaces.[22] And then, in September, Baxter hosted an all-hands meeting where he presented, in great detail, the overall reorganization of the company.

Within weeks of the launch, a new client and an existing client began to use some of Huge's new products, sold to them for fixed product prices, to bring about improvement in results and growth.

By any standard, progress was rapid in this early phase of Huge's transformation. This reflected the quick adoption of the concepts and language from the company's engagement with TBMC.

CHAPTER 8
HUGE'S PRODUCTIZATION STRATEGY

*"**Warranty.** These HUGE products are designed to accelerate client growth. Check the labels to confirm your order for experience transformation, technology realization and growth creation."*

Credit: Dennis Flad

The productization team created a tagline that tied Huge's product line strategy to the company's new mission: 'Products need Problems.'

Products exist to solve client problems. That is their *raison d'être*. As Huge embarked on developing a new line of products, it had to crystallize what kinds of client problems it wanted to solve, and what kinds of products it needed to develop. Each product would be associated with one of the three front doors: Experience Transformation, Technology Realization, and Growth Creation.

The overriding notion was that if it developed products tailored for each front door, Huge would be able to solve the problems associated with each door.

Continuing with the TBMC productization process, the Polpo teams set out to more clearly define the front doors and, sometime later, begin a process that would lead to the development of a suite of products for each drawer. At the beginning of the product-development process, after the doors had been selected and named, product teams were appointed and aligned to each of them. TBMC provided the product development templates and processes, including pricing methodology and models. This work was led by De Bonis, Manning and Transformation Management lead Matt Creer, in close partnership with executives associated with each of the front doors. They included Brian Fletcher (Group VP, Technology), Brian Donovan (Group VP, Strategy), and Irina Kondrashova (Group VP, Strategy). In addition, industry analysts, and even some clients, were consulted as part of the process.

Eventually, the term front door was changed to 'growth gateway.' As Manning explained, "Future clients will come to us because they need experience transformation, technology realization, or growth creation, not because they have projects or briefs that they want us to execute. These new growth gateways are the portals where we will meet and greet our future customers. Products will replace services; we will abandon the selling of services and replace it with the selling of products."

The doorways, and their underlying product portfolios, were defined as such:

- **Experience Transformation** is designed for Chief Marketing Officers, Chief Experience Officers, and Chief Design Officers. *"We accelerate growth by helping to bring about fundamental improvements in customer experience."* Clients needing Experience Transformation enter Huge via this gateway, which has a number of longer-term programs and products to help solve their customer experience problems.
- **Technology Realization** is designed for Chief Technology Officers, Chief Digital Officers, and Chief Information Officers. *"We help unlock trapped value in technology for the benefit of people."* Clients needing Technology Realization enter Huge via this gateway to use the agency's technology realization programs and products.

84

- **Growth Creation** is designed for Chief Executive Officers, Chief Experience Officers, and Chief Strategy Officers. *"We help uncover and capitalize on new sources of value."* Clients needing growth enter Huge via this gateway to use the assembled growth creation programs and products.

This product-first approach means that Huge has to do a thoughtful job of describing its products. These descriptions are critical for the development of new client relationships.

PRODUCTIZATION FRAMEWORK

Huge was committed to following the TBMC playbook for the development of products. Once the names of the three growth gateways were determined, the playbook required the development of three *client performance challenges* that fit each gateway.

For **Experience Transformation**, for example, the three performance challenges created by Huge were described as follows, using the voice of a potential client:

1. **Audience.** *"I need to attract the next generation of buyers — whoever they are — to drive strong affinity for our brand and to increase our sales."*

2. **Spend.** *"I need to optimize my spend across channels and journeys to make the most of every marketing dollar."*

3. **Campaign.** *"I need help to execute a tent-pole campaign, not only to drive sales but to build affinity for my brand as well."*

Technology Realization, Huge's second gateway, addressed a different set of performance challenges:

1. **Reinvention.** *"Our technology organization is stuck in the past. We are looking for a partner to help us reinvent our technology, and develop high-value capabilities and expertise, to deliver more value."*

2. **Modernization.** *"Our organization has vast 'technological debt' in its architecture, and we are looking for a partner to help modernize it to enable the organization to outpace the competition."*

3. **Roadmap.** *"Our business is at a crossroads as we look to evaluate and upgrade the technology and systems that fuel our organization. Unfortunately, our team is stuck, and we do not know how to take that first step on our journey."*

Finally, **Growth Creation**, the most fluid of the three growth gateways, describes its three performance challenges this way:

1. **New products.** *"I need to rapidly define high-value new products and services, and scale them in a way that will maximize my ROI."*

2. **Customers and markets.** *"I need to rapidly identify, reach and deliver my products and services to new, high-value customers and markets."*

3. **Business model transformation.** *"I need to sustainably transform my business model and my organization to generate more customer and business value."*

The effort to name the three growth gateways and define the corresponding performance challenges was an intense and taxing undertaking for the Huge team. TBMC provided the framework and the encouragement, but the actual work was done by the company's productization team. De Bonis and Manning led this effort, but other executives were enlisted to move it forward, and expert reinforcements were brought in from time to time to broaden their capabilities.

Naming the growth gateways and writing the performance challenges for each was a first priority. Subsequently, the team faced an additional and complicated step: each performance challenge needed 'five drawers,' each representing one step of a client's value journey, with each drawer containing a single product. Each drawer had a name and purpose. The productization team would need to develop and name the products that would be housed in each drawer.

The five steps of a client's value journey are listed below, with their associated drawers.

1. Drawer #1: **Disrupt Behaviors**

2. Drawer #2: **Develop a Framework**

3. Drawer #3: **Design the Experience**

4. Drawer #4: **Deploy Capabilities**

5. Drawer #5: **Drive Results**

With three growth gateways, three performance challenges per gateway, and five drawers per challenge, Huge would have 45 drawers containing 45 products. (Later, Huge's language would be simplified, and 'drawers' would be abandoned as an unnecessary term.) Each of the three growth gateways would have 15 products.

The productization team, with its fluid membership, divided up the product development workload, assigning growth gateways and performance challenges. Team members drafted product descriptions and then reconvened as a group to review the nomenclature. The product descriptions were then edited by the group. The job was completed once the productization team reached consensus on the individual product descriptions and Baxter had signed off on them.

The outcome of the work was the naming of the 45 products in the Huge product portfolio. They are shown below, gateway by gateway, with their thumbnail descriptions:

EXPERIENCE TRANSFORMATION GROWTH GATEWAY

CHALLENGES →	PERFORMANCE CHALLENGE #1	PERFORMANCE CHALLENGE #2	PERFORMANCE CHALLENGE #3
DRAWERS (CLIENT VALUE JOURNEY) ↓	ATTRACT THE NEXT GENERATION OF BUYERS	OPTIMIZE SPEND	EXECUTE A TENT-POLE CAMPAIGN
DISRUPT BEHAVIORS	CATEGORY CRASHER Identify ways to disrupt your category	BRAND VALUE IGNITOR Ignite business value through disruptive brand strategy	EXPERIENCE ECOSYSTEM MULTIPLIER Build a strategy to get the most from your brand ecosystem
DEVELOP A FRAMEWORK	OPPORTUNITY PRIORITIZER Analyze and prioritize your efforts for impact	VISION CREATOR Galvanize your organization around a vision	VISION ENABLER Create a plan to activate and accelerate your vision
DESIGN THE EXPERIENCE	OPPORTUNITY VALIDATOR Rapidly pilot and assess new initiatives in market	BRAND MAGNETIZER Build magnetic brand experiences across your ecosystem	EXPERIENCE FLAGSHIP Build a hero experience that sets a new bar
DEPLOY CAPABILITIES	EXPERIENCE REALIZER Successfully execute your newly designed experiences	CHANGE CATALYZER Transform your people, operations, and culture	EXPERIENCE ACCELERATION ENGAGER Accelerate the value of your customer experience investments
DRIVE RESULTS	BRAND VALUE EXTENDER Build a rigorous case to target new brand value pools	IMPACT ACCELERATOR Scale and supercharge your assets across the business	CREATIVE CAPITAL ACCELERATOR Track and optimize your organization's transformation

TECHNOLOGY REALIZATION GROWTH GATEWAY

CHALLENGES →	PERFORMANCE CHALLENGE #1	PERFORMANCE CHALLENGE #2	PERFORMANCE CHALLENGE #3
DRAWERS (CLIENT VALUE JOURNEY) ↓	REINVENT IMAGE AND DEVELOP HIGH-VALUE CAPABILITIES AND EXPERTISE TO DELIVER MORE VALUE	MODERNIZE ARCHITECTURE TO ENABLE CLIENTS TO OUTPACE COMPETITION	EVALUATE AND UPGRADE TECHNOLOGY AND SYSTEMS
DISRUPT BEHAVIORS	**TRAPPED VALUE LOCATOR** Identify the trapped value in your technology investments	**FUTURE GROWTH PRIORITIZER** Identify where technology can power future growth	**LEADERSHIP ALIGNER** Galvanize alignment with your leadership on your vision for technology
DEVELOP A FRAMEWORK	**PEOPLE-FIRST ARCHITECTURE** Transform your technology for a people-centric architecture	**DECISION PATHFINDER** Create consensus on where to build, buy, or partner within your technology ecosystem	**TECHNOLOGY INVESTMENT CASE** Quantify, and advocate for the impact of, your people-first architecture
DESIGN THE EXPERIENCE	**PRIORITY PATHWAYS** Prioritize initiatives, creating clarity while optimizing ROI	**PROGRAM ACTIVATOR** Implement specific programs with highly efficient sequencing	**TRANSFORMATION JUMPSTART** Jolt key transformational initiatives and programs into action
DEPLOY CAPABILITIES	**AGILITY ACCELERATOR** Maximize the velocity and performance of your teams	**PERFORMANCE ACCELERATOR** Rapidly move the dial on your critical metrics	**CAPABILITY BUILDER** Rapidly build new capabilities within your organization
DRIVE RESULTS	**LIVING INTELLIGENCE VALUE ENGINE** Measure and track your performance and value	**NEXT OPPORTUNITY IDENTIFIER** Identify new opportunities to accelerate your impact	**INNOVATION EVALUATOR** Guide critical innovation investment decisions across your portfolio

GROWTH CREATION GATEWAY

CHALLENGES →	PERFORMANCE CHALLENGE #1	PERFORMANCE CHALLENGE #2	PERFORMANCE CHALLENGE #3
DRAWERS (CLIENT VALUE JOURNEY) ↓	DEFINE HIGH-VALUE NEW PRODUCTS AND SERVICES AND SCALE THEM IN A WAY THAT WILL MAXIMIZE ROI	IDENTIFY AND DELIVER PRODUCTS AND SERVICES TO NEW, HIGH-VALUE CUSTOMERS AND MARKETS	SUSTAINABLY TRANSFORM BUSINESS MODEL AND ORGANIZATION TO GENERATE MORE CUSTOMER AND BUSINESS VALUE
DISRUPT BEHAVIORS	**HUGE MOVES** Define new and radical growth strategies for your business	**NEW HORIZON VALIDATOR** Refine and quantify an existing growth idea	**BUSINESS READINESS DIAGNOSTIC** Identify your growth capabilities and blockers
DEVELOP A FRAMEWORK	**CUSTOMER FINDER** Find and define existing and new high-growth customers	**BUSINESS MODEL BUILDER** Create a new business model to accelerate growth	**GROWTH OFFERINGS CREATOR** Define new, high-value offerings
DESIGN THE EXPERIENCE	**CHANGE ENABLER** Mobilize your organization to drive change and growth	**COMMERCIAL MODELER** Model the commercial value of new growth offerings	**FLIGHT PLANNER** Create a plan to deliver new offerings quickly
DEPLOY CAPABILITIES	**MARKET TESTER** Launch an in-market, minimum-value product	**CAPABILITIES KICKSTARTER** Build new capabilities to enable business growth	**MARKET MOTIVATOR** Attract customers to your new growth offerings
DRIVE RESULTS	**FUTURE SCENARIO MODELER** Identify disruption indictors and your next-best actions	**VENTURE ACCELERATOR** Scale your growth offerings quickly and efficiently	**ADVANTAGE MULTIPLIER** Identify new growth to leverage recent successes

I asked Baxter if he thought Huge really needed 45 products. Didn't this create a burdensome development effort for the productization team? Wasn't the team's creativity being pushed to the limit to identify and describe so many different offerings? And would clients really have such an extensive, granular list of needs in the first place? Baxter explained:

> I could have simplified this. I could have told TBMC at the beginning that we would work with three doors, three performance challenges ,and only three drawers, and mathematically this would have led to 27 products, rather than 45. That might have eased the pressure on our productization team. But who is to say that 27 products is right and 45 is too many? We began productization with zero products, and our team had no experience. We brought in TBMC because they had extensive productization experience, and the 45-product framework they provided was their recommended framework. I reasoned that it made complete sense to follow their guidance, rather than tinker with it from a position of ignorance. We hired them for a reason, and we followed their guidance.
>
> We understood from the beginning that these 45 products were theoretical products until they had an actual track record with clients. Experience will prove that some of the products are neither effective nor salable, and we will drop them.

PRODUCT PRICING

The next scheduled phase of the productization work was the pricing piece, whereby each product would be given a fixed price, based on the value of each to customers, and the number, seniority, expertise, and duration of resources required for implementation. Baxter and his finance team wanted to ensure that each product could deliver a healthy margin.

One thing was non-negotiable: each product would have a fixed price. Gone was the concept that Huge would discuss full-time equivalent timesheet numbers, man-hours per head, billing rates per head, overhead rates, or profit margins with customers. Instead, the company would charge a fixed price for each product. A typical engagement might require multiple products, each with a unique price. The price of a client engagement would be the sum of the prices of the individual products.

If the products delivered on their promise, and clients achieved the improved performance that they sought, Huge's product fees would be a tiny fraction of achieved results.

Productization was a key element of the long-term transformation strategy, supporting the company's revised mission and pricing strategy.

All that remained was to try out the products with new customers, and hope for a track record of success over the next few years.

CHAPTER 9
REORGANIZATION

"We're moving our house to a better neighborhood."
Credit: Dennis Flad

Throughout the transformation process, Baxter and his leadership team were mindful of the need to communicate with employees, keeping them abreast of progress and assuring them that the proposed future of the company would be positive and enriching. This was not at all simple. The transformation was taking place as two years of Covid disruption continued to wax, wane, and flare up again, with remote working, the threat of reduced client activity, and twists and turns almost weekly that no one could anticipate.

The trade press carried news of many agencies downsizing as the pandemic ground on.

It was in the middle of all this that Baxter, the young Australian with a background in media, had parachuted in as Huge's new chief executive. Although he'd made a positive initial impression through his efforts to remotely meet all employees, and seemed like an open communicator who wasn't afraid to speak his mind, he remained an unknown. Employees had every right to feel insecure about their futures in a Covid-wracked world, with an industry in transition, a changing company, and a new CEO.

Around the world, in each of its 12 offices, Huge's Creative Department was by far the largest operation, accounting for more than a quarter of all employees. As mentioned earlier, Creative chief Jason Musante had left a few months after Baxter's arrival. Most employees should have known by this point that Baxter was leading the company into a major transformation. Would Huge be disinvesting from creativity? What would the future hold for several hundred creative employees worldwide, and the many colleagues who worked side-by-side with them? Indeed, what was in store for each and every Huge employee?

Among the changes that would most directly affect staff were any shifts in office organization, especially if they involved downsizing. Although most employees had not visited their offices for nearly two years during Covid lockdowns, they still 'belonged' to Brooklyn, to London, to Toronto, to Berkeley, or to other offices around the world. Offices were anchors and foundations. Employees were recruited by local office executives, and office presidents were the most senior executives most of them knew. The presidents gave speeches, announced new clients, promoted employees, and organized parties. Employees were assigned to clients managed by their offices, and they received their monthly pay from office payroll systems. They received performance reviews and promotions from local execs. Offices celebrated new clients, and locals went out for drinks with one another. Offices grounded the professional and personal lives of employees in the geographic areas where they lived and worked.

Baxter knew early on that he wanted to turn Huge into a single global enterprise. This would see the leadership team taking greater control of the company, with global client development, global allocation of people to clients, and global product development. This would require a change in the roles of office presidents, and careful preparation of employees to see themselves as part of a worldwide group of talented resources, rather than staff in one office or another. The office change would be dramatic for every Huge employee.

Before communicating anything about a change in office structure, Baxter felt he had to describe in broad strokes the commercial strategy that would justify any reconfiguration. Thus far, TBMC's presence, and the elements of Project Polpo, were unknown to most employees. The three doors approach and productization efforts were also invisible — they had little relevance for most employees, at least at this early stage of the game.

In February 2022, Baxter organized an all-hands meeting where he laid out what he called a 'product and services update.' Not until seven months later would he follow this up with an announcement about the reorganization of the company and the changed status of local offices.

The content of the product and services update was carefully worked out in advance with ELT members. They agreed that the employee presentation needed to be short and simple — communicated remotely, with a short video to provide visual support. Baxter prefaced his presentation by noting that he was describing a product strategy, not a company reorganization... although he did set the stage for additional changes to come.

*Please remember today what I'm taking you through is how we organize our products for clients. It's the way that we package up what we do as a company, so clients can understand what we do and navigate the product offering that Huge has across the board. **This is not the structure of the company.** Do not get confused by this and think, 'Oh, this is how we're going to be structured as an organization.' It isn't that. That will be coming soon. We're doing that work right now. We don't want to complete that work until we understand the products that we'll be selling. Once we've done the product work, I'll be giving you an update on a new structure.*

He also felt a need to address the critical issue of creativity. Would the new mission and new products mean that Huge was disinvesting on the creative side?

> *So, before I explain our productization strategy, let's talk about the principles that guided us in how we've gone about doing what you're about to see. The first is, **creativity is at the core of everything that we do. It will be woven into the way that you navigate the business, but also, more importantly, the products that we offer clients. Creativity is still our core point of differentiation. It lives in everything, and it is fundamentally the thing that makes Huge unique and different from companies like consultancies.** That is not going to change. In fact, that's going to accelerate under the new approach that we're taking as a business.*

He then moved on to a description of the new Huge, using a video that showed the company as a house under renovation. It would have three front doors, named Experience Transformation, Technology Realization, and Growth Creation. He elaborated on the nature and purpose of each doorway. Who were the clients who would come in through each door? What did they need? How would the company serve them? He described the CMOs, CXOs, and CIOs who were struggling, with less than complete success, to deliver topline growth. After this, he described the need to move the entire Huge house out of its ad agency neighborhood and into a better neighborhood — one with higher house prices and better neighbors. The video showed the Huge house being picked up, as if by a powerful tornado, and zooming across town, into a neighborhood with nicer homes and larger lots. He described the trade-up:

> *What we want to do is to lift our house up, and we want to move our house from the brand and digital agencies' neighborhood, where it now is, and drop our house into a new neighborhood called the growth acceleration neighborhood. That neighborhood is a less crowded neighborhood, and the house prices are higher. So, we're not only going to have less competition, but we're going to be able to get a better price for what we do than what we get today.*

Following his presentation, there was a vigorous Q&A session, where employees seemed to show that the basic product and services messaging had been effectively delivered and was understood.

Baxter closed the meeting by thanking everyone for their many contributions. It had been a tough year, requiring many sacrifices. In recognition of that, he announced that he was giving an immediate $1,000 bonus to each and every employee, as a way of saying 'thank you' for the support, commitment, and successes Huge had enjoyed in 2021.

———————

Seven months later, in September 2022, following the productization team's development of its suite of 45 products — and with a few new and current clients actually using the new offerings — Baxter and the ELT were prepared to implement a company reorganization and formally announce it to employees.

There was more to the reorganization than changing the status and concept of offices. The global company needed a new structure to manage clients, its global talent and its products. But it also still needed physical spaces in key geographic areas: places employees could go for things like working and socializing and career development, even if attendance was voluntary rather than obligatory. What Huge did not need were offices as profit centers — the mini-agencies from the past, which fragmented the overall business and diluted its effectiveness.

As far as office attendance was concerned, a poll of employees had shown that three-quarters did not want to return to the offices post-Covid. Baxter could see the writing on the wall: remote working was a permanent reality, and the sooner the company learned to live with its implications, the better. And so, in late 2021 he announced a 'fully flexible' work location policy. Henceforth, physically showing up at a brick & mortar location for the workday would be voluntary.

The offices would be converted into 'experience centers' for employees. Huge would continue to invest in new spaces, though. It was leaving its tired Brooklyn office, for example, and creating a major new space in the historic Brooklyn Navy Yard, a revitalized center for urban innovation.

POD ORGANIZATION

To manage its business, the company would organize itself globally into three 'pods,' each focused on one of three priorities. There would be Client Pods for client development and management; Craft Pods for talent/expertise development and management; and Product Pods for product development and management.

In the new organization, a discipline called Talent Craft would have an especially important role. Along with the usual HR functions, like recruiting, it would add Team Design, focused on assembling client teams and allocating them to Client Pods. This would be done on a global basis, from the center, rather than carried out in the old office-by-office way. The hope was that Team Design would ensure that the right kinds of people were assigned to individual clients and Client Pods, matching skills with needs from anywhere in the world, and delivering the greatest value to the customer.

The term 'pod' was meant to signal Huge's change in organization and philosophy. In today's parlance, a pod is neither a department nor a team, both of which (in most organizations) are hierarchical in nature, with clear bosses and subordinates who take direction from the top.

Baxter and De Bonis developed the company's high-level pod concept, and Manning helped flesh it out for implementation.

The pod structure was expected to be more collaborative and agile, bringing together groups of individuals from different disciplines, combining their know-how to build custom products and design innovative solutions for clients.

CLIENT PODS

Client Pods (CPs) provide the structure where client work is carried out, with multidisciplinary teams coming together to think, collaborate and do their best work to drive growth for the customer. Baxter organized the company into four Global CPs, each led by a former office or regional client leader. The CPs were named after key dates related to Huge's history:

- CP99 represents the company's founding in 1999. Its president is Blake Wirht. This client portfolio is made up entirely of engagements for a large, single global client.

- CP05 represents the employee anniversary woodman's axe. Its president is Megan Malli. This pod is made up of clients and staff from Huge's legacy London, Toronto, and Midwestern US (Chicago and Detroit) offices.
- CP10 represents what Huge calls "The Goat." When an employee reaches 10 years of service, he or she is given a month-long sabbatical, or Go Away Time (GOAT). This pod comprises clients from the legacy Southeast (DC and Atlanta) and West (Oakland and LA) regions. Jon Judah, who had been the Southeast region president, is responsible for CP10.
- CP72 represents Dock 72, which will be the home of Huge's experience center at the Brooklyn Navy Yard. It pulls together clients from Huge's legacy Brooklyn office. Matt Weiss, formerly the president of Brooklyn, heads up CP72.

Each Client Pod is expected to carry out client work anywhere in the world, leveraging the right resources, wherever they might be located. Each Client Pod leader is accountable for the health and growth of their respective client portfolios. Health and growth are the key metrics; they are not measured or managed as profit centers.

Specific KPIs for the Client Pods involve: client success (business outcomes); Huge revenues and client retention rates; and client/ team satisfaction, as gauged by customer satisfaction survey tools like the Net Promoter Score (NPS), and The Referral Rating (TRR).

Along with the four Client Pod leaders, each pod includes permanently assigned senior executives representing cross-craft disciplines, like Client Partners (account management), Operations, Program Delivery, Strategy, Creative, and Technology. These senior cross-craft leaders are broadly accountable for ensuring that experts assigned to clients from their disciplines are effectively collaborating on behalf of those clients.

The other people who work in Client Pods are known as global craft members, assigned by Team Design to specific clients within the pods. These individuals are temporary members of the Client Pods, but permanent members of their separate and respective Craft Pods (described below). They represent the creative, strategy, technology, and data & insights disciplinary centers within Huge. They are allocated to Client Pods by Team Design to do specific client work. Over time, these individual assignments may be modified as a result of changes in Huge's client base. Thus, each Client Pod has a combination of permanent senior leaders, representing each of the crafts, and global craft members who carry out the actual client work.

HUGE'S CLIENT POD STRUCTURE

CRAFT PODS

Craft Pods are the disciplinary centers within Huge, headed by senior executives who are specialists in their craft. These leaders are principally responsible for training, developing and mentoring the individuals in their crafts. Craft Pods are the permanent homes for every employee. Their leaders are responsible for establishing highly capable crafts whose members are engaged in continuous learning and improvement in professional capabilities. Craft leaders are expected to evaluate the skill levels of their employees, and engage in recruiting and training to assure that Huge has the right capacity and capabilities for its clients. The 12 Craft Pods are as follows:

1. Client Partnership Craft

2. Program Delivery Craft

3. Operations Craft

4. DE&I Craft

5. Legal Craft

6. Creative Craft, with specializations in Experience Innovation, Brand Design & Content, Products & Services, and Business Design

7. Strategy Craft: Business & Data Consulting, Brand Strategy, Experience Strategy, and Product Management

8. Technology Craft: Technology Strategy, Transformative Technology, Architecture & Delivery, User Interface Engineering, Platform Systems & Backend, and Quality Assurance

9. Data & Insights Craft: Business & Data Consulting, Data Science & Analytics, Insights, and Data Products

10. Growth Craft: Business Development, Reputation & Communications, and Growth Operations

11. Finance Craft: Financial Planning & Analysis, Accounting, Huge Habitats, IT, and Client Finance

12. Talent Craft: Talent Partnering, Recruiting & Team Design, Huge Experiences Team, and Organizational Development & Effectiveness

PRODUCT PODS

The Product Pods are the third organizational structure that serves clients. The pods carry out product development activities and help Client Partners sell products to new and existing clients. There are three Product Pods, each associated with one of the three doors (growth gateways): Experience Transformation, Technology Realization, and Growth Creation.

The Product Pod is collaboratively led by CPO De Bonis, plus an Operations & Solutions Officer and a Commercial Finance Officer.

Product Pod KPIs include product sales, product training outcomes, and product quality, as measured by achievement of promised outcomes.

The pod organizational scheme created many Huge executive positions that would have a hand in defining and carrying out the specific work for clients. Permanent Client Pod members — like Client Partners, and Craft executives in Operations, Program Delivery, Strategy and Technology — are expected to cooperatively define the work around specific products, and they bring in global Creatives, Strategists, Technologists, and Data & Insights resources. All the work involves the use of named products from one or more of the Product Pods, and product specialists are assigned to client teams to bring an expert point of view on product capabilities and uses.

Although the pod concept leans heavily on the notion of collaboration, rather than hierarchy, it is clear that such a diverse group of individuals could squabble about how client needs could be best met. Who gets to decide what products should be allocated, and what crafts are most essential? How do the client partners, craft practitioners, and product specialists collaborate on a common vision? Recognizing this, Huge was developing an accountability framework to define how the client-facing people, craft experts and product specialists would work with another.

There was consensus among Baxter and the ELT that Client Partners would have the ultimate responsibility for client success and growth, and that the other Client Pod members and assigned craft and product experts would work within an accountability framework that would see Client Partners in this light.

DE&I considerations were an additional, important factor. Baxter and the ELT put progress in diversity and inclusion at the top of their list of reorganization priorities, giving Toni Lowe, the Global DE&I Executive, a strong voice within the leadership team. "We believe that our work towards being a diverse and antiracist company is never done," she said. "We are not satisfied with the DE&I makeup of the company. We will continue our commitment to staying accountable, and being held accountable, to make progress across all levels, including leadership, at Huge. There is much to do to ensure that we have a diverse talent pool at every level of the organization."

Lowe came to Huge shortly before Baxter's arrival, having worked for more than a decade as a DE&I executive at EY, McAfee, and USAA. Working with Baxter, she has helped ensure that each member of leadership team has clearly defined DE&I performance objectives, structured to increase the number of diverse employees among the pods and at company headquarters.

HOW WILL THIS IMPACT EMPLOYEES?

In announcing the reorganization in September 2022, Huge simultaneously issued a 21-page Transformation FAQ document (see Appendix) that outlined the structure and details of the restructuring.

The document attempted to answer questions the ELT thought would be top-of-mind across the workforce. For instance, the final four pages focused on 'How Will this Impact Me,' given that the reorganization would create employee concern amid all the changes.

One principle ran through the internal messaging: Huge would seek minimum disruption in 2022 as it implemented its reorganization. Radical as it was, the company would not make changes just for the sake of change, and there would be a continuity of practices wherever possible.

As we will cover in more detail later in the book, the FAQ provided answers to the following questions:

1. How will this reorganization change my day-to-day work activity?

2. If I currently work on a retainer-based client, will this go away under our new operating model?

3. How will this reorganization help me to do better work or gain new skills?

4. As a global organization, will salaries by level be consistent regardless of where people live?

5. Can I live and work from anywhere?

6. With regions going away and crafts consolidating, does this limit my opportunities for autonomy?

7. Does anyone's immediate supervisor/manager change with this reorganization?

8. Are Craft Pod managers still responsible for the onboarding, training, and overall career growth of their direct reports?

9. Updates used to occur at office-level meetings. How will we find out about new clients and upcoming projects?

10. Are there any job title or career path changes associated with this reorganization?

11. If my title or role changes, am I entitled to a raise?

12. Will Huge be providing new job descriptions and ways of working for any roles under the new organizational structure?

13. Will we need to adopt new skills or trades as part of this reorganization?

14. How will teams be designed globally? How will Team Design know my capabilities and how to deploy me?

15. What guardrails will be put in place to support a healthy work/life balance for those working on projects with team members spread across multiple time zones?

———————

Within two weeks of announcing the reorganization, Huge launched a redesigned website. Gone was the picture of the axe-wielding employee and the fragmented messages of the old site. These were replaced by a new logo, a new color scheme and a simple message about Huge's new mission:

About you. Not about us.

You're a progressive leader, looking to transform your company and realise its full potential. You're open to new ideas, new technologies and new partners. You're a believer in the power of creativity. You're looking for a respectful sparring partner. You're obsessed with results.

You're the client we've been looking for.

→ Let's talk

Your growth. Our expertise.

As a business leader, you know all too well about the relentless focus on delivering results for your company. And that's where Huge comes in. Our deep and expansive expertise has proven, time and time again, that we can achieve powerful outcomes for our clients.

So, whether you're tasked with transforming your customer experiences, unlocking the power of technology within your organisation, or stimulating new growth with brave new initiatives, we're here to deliver the results you need.

By the end of September 2022 — now a year into the transformation process, with a revised mission, a new set of products and a reorganized company structure — Huge was on its way to operating as an entirely reinvented company.

CHAPTER 10
MANAGING RESOURCES
— GLOBALLY

*"And that's how we do global
resource allocation!"*

Credit: Dennis Flad

Before the reorganization, each office president managed (or
attempted to manage) office profitability to a certain required margin level. This required developing and maintaining clients, as well
as having the right number of office-based expert resources. Office
revenues — less office costs, including salaries, overhead, and direct
costs — were calculated to meet the margin target for the fiscal year.
Every office had to stand on its own: Huge's overall performance was
the sum of its offices, less the additional staff costs and overhead
associated with the corporate headquarters.

Offices that missed financial targets would need to take cost-cutting actions, such as reducing full-time equivalent headcount and implementing hiring freezes and travel restrictions. Office headcount reductions would be made even if the targeted resources could theoretically be used elsewhere.

In the past, Huge had neither the overall data nor the organizational processes whereby cross-office staffing might be implemented — there was no generally accepted mechanism to coordinate global staffing. Previously, the company didn't even think of itself in global terms; it was an organization of 12 separate offices.

The office profit-center system could create a double whammy during difficult times — one hit on the office side, where downsizing would weaken staffing dedicated to current clients and put stress on remaining employees, and the other, an impact on Huge, where good talent would be forced out of the company, even the talent could be used elsewhere. Strategically, this was a lose-lose proposition for the company's long-term viability and relevance.

With this office-based system, the profitability of individual clients in each office could vary considerably, as long as overall office profitability targets were met. Certain clients might generate superior profits, well above the objectives, while others could have depressed margins or even be money-losing. As long as the overall office margin equaled or exceeded the target, financial objectives would be met, and this would constitute success for top management. Client-by-client profitability was a secondary concern. In many cases, unprofitable accounts, resulting from unsuccessful fee negotiations and overly demanding scopes of work, were explained away with, 'That's just the way things are.' Clients, rather than the company, were seen as the authors of unprofitable or marginal engagements.

In early 2017, Huge hired Mimi Moore, who'd been at DigitasLBi (later renamed Digitas) in New York, to organize a cross-office resource allocation system. Her mission was to identify underutilized people within the Huge network and make them available to offices whose clients were understaffed. She described the challenge:

I entered an office-based system where some of the leaders did not even know one another, and they did not normally talk to one other.

So, I had to become a human solution to this problem — flying around the country, visiting Huge offices, getting to know the people, building relationships, those kinds of things. I was the exception to our siloed structure. It was hard. I would provide a senior visual designer from Atlanta for a Brooklyn-based need, for example, and later hear from Brooklyn that the designer did not meet their unique requirements. This was hard on the employees who had this experience.

The change of office status and the commitment to manage clients and resources from the center was the transformation solution, along with determining staffing needs for each of Huge's 45 products. Since new clients would be buying one or several products, and the necessary resources for each of these products could be determined in advance, staffing for clients could be managed in a logical fashion. Products were now sold at prices that made them profitable, given the resources that were built into their structures.

The major complication in doing this in the real world is that it involves reassigning people out of a global pool on an ongoing basis, based on availability, skill levels, client needs, and other practical considerations. It is one thing to have a suite of products supported by predetermined, standardized staffing levels, and another matter entirely to actually find and assign individuals from around the world. Surely, this would require a dynamic process that would have to be reviewed and managed at least monthly.

This dynamic allocation process requires a comprehensive database of employee and client-project information, little of which existed at the company before the transformation. There were countless considerations. Who are the employees in each of the geographic areas, and what are their skill levels, past experiences, strengths, weaknesses, and leadership abilities? What are their current client assignments, and how critical is each individual to the achievement of client objectives? What client projects are currently running, and what projects are planned for the rest of the fiscal year? How long will these projects run? What skill levels will future projects require? Are the required skill levels available from the global talent pool? When is each employee available for reassignment to new projects?

Moore has since been promoted to an ELT-level position as Managing Director, Recruiting, and Team Design, overseeing the project-driven assignment of employees on a global level. "Our hope is," she said, "if you are in the creative craft, you can work on any creative work that takes place in London, or New York, or Atlanta, or Oakland, or anywhere. It should not matter where the clients' offices are. If you work at Huge, in any craft, your skills and tools and processes should be uniform within each craft on a global basis. That's where we have to get to. We need to develop Salesforce, Mavenlink, and Adaptive, our various systems, to house the data we need to carry out our staffing responsibilities. That is the track we are currently on."

Global allocation of employees to new work in the Client Pods is rather complex at this early stage in the transformation. Moore characterized it this way:

> The Client Partner and the Program Delivery person know their clients best, and they're tasked with achieving long-term growth and prosperity with their clients. They need the right resources to do this job. On the other hand, the Craft Leaders own and mentor the expert people in their crafts, and they have a better idea about the skills and capabilities of their individuals. So, when we serve up a list of recommendations, we have to go to the craft leaders to get their approval, and this takes some time. The Client Pod leaders, who are under client pressure to staff up work quickly, are frustrated with the amount of time this currently takes. This process is much slower than what it was when we had offices, and Office Presidents who were clearly in charge of clients and their office people.

However, she acknowledged that these problems are not unique: "They're fundamental within resource management, and in time, changes will certainly be made to make our allocation system run much smoother."

CHAPTER 11
CRITICAL REVIEW

The fly-on-the-wall renders a judgment.
Credit: Dennis Flad

By October 2022, most of the transformation elements were in place, 16 months after Baxter's appointment as CEO. Huge had: adopted a new mission; productized its client offerings; globalized its operations by eliminating a dozen office profit centers; adopted a global 3-dimensional matrix organization (clients, crafts, products) around four client pods; and begun the process of allocating expert talent to clients by a centralized Team Design craft. Furthermore, Baxter and the ELT had communicated openly with employees about the transformation.

Although there were many tweaks expected in the coming months and years, the transformation elements were in place. What was now required to continue the process was to convert existing clients, develop new clients, and then follow through with the allocation of talent, delivery of improved growth, and expansion of client relationships.

Understandably, this operational phase would generate new learnings and insights about product effectiveness, organizational design and process requirements, and ongoing changes could certainly be expected as the transformation gained traction and evolved.

As things moved into the operational phase, one short year after the first executive retreat, and before any real progress had been seen, some ELT members were somewhat anxious. Would the transformation really work? Were their key choices correct? Were there other alternatives they should have considered? What further changes would be necessary in the coming months and years? These concerns were understandable, I thought, in view of the scope and intensity of the transformation effort. It had been exhausting for the leadership team, working all-out to run the business while delivering innovations for the Polpo project.

The ELT now had a bit of breathing room to reflect on the changes it had put in place.

Predictably, they wondered what kind of a future they'd created for themselves, and how they could make it even better.

I had my own thoughts about what Baxter and the team had accomplished. The transformation went well beyond what I'd expected would happen. Here, for the record, are my thoughts.

MISSION: ACCELERATED GROWTH FOR CLIENTS

It would be hard to make a case for any mission other than helping clients accelerate their growth. Like it or not, corporations (Huge's clients) are driven by the concept that they exist to increase value for shareholders, and value is defined by improved topline growth and profitability. Increased share price is the measure of shareholder value, and that's driven principally by current financial performance and expectations of improvements in future growth and profitability.

Topline growth has been embarrassingly low for many major advertisers since the financial crisis of 2009, and CMOs bear some responsibility for this. The massive marketing investments they made in digital and social channels have not yielded hoped-for outcomes. CMOs have suffered the consequences — they come and go, turning over at twice the rate as the CEOs for whom they work. They've allowed the relationships with their media and creative agencies to deteriorate over time, seeing many of them decline from marketing-focused partnerships to procurement-driven vendorships. Illogically, their agency relationships are now based on 'We want you to do a lot of stuff that we've thought about, and do it for the lowest fee possible,' rather than 'Help us to figure out how to accelerate growth.'

Huge cannot rely on new clients to ask for work that focuses on achieving improved results — that's not how the industry works (although it should). Instead, Huge needs to take the initiative by stating: "We are in the business of helping our clients achieve improved growth rates. If that's what you want and need, we are the right partner for you. If not — if you're looking for a firm that will crank out a list of low-cost deliverables — you need to look elsewhere."

Baxter mobilized his 20-person top management team around this accelerated growth strategy during that initial leadership retreat, just months after his arrival as the new CEO. Defining the new mission was the principal purpose of the session. There was no discussion of productization or reorganization — that would come later, once the TBMC engagement was well under way and the Polpo change management program had been defined.

The executives who attended the 2021 retreat could not have anticipated all the changes the revised mission would generate. At the time, they bought into the new vision and breathed a sigh of relief that Huge had a new CEO who encouraged them to adopt a new wordview, and who brought charisma and personal energy to the table. After their experience with the four previous CEOs, and little in the way of improved results to show for it, ELT members were eager to try something new, and the new and improved mission made a great deal of sense.

Once mobilized around the mission, the executives were insiders in the transformation effort, and each would be called to carry out his or her responsibilities with energy and commitment. Without a unified management team, Baxter could not have dared to initiate a transformation as dramatic as the one that would unfold during 2021 and 2022.

PRODUCTIZATION

Once TBMC completed its diagnosis of Huge's client base, and made its case for change, the transformation shifted to the productization phase, detailed in Chapter 8. As described, this would lead to the creation of 45 products, each with a fixed price.

This was an internally managed process that mobilized executives from many disciplines within the company. The process was designed to marry the executives' knowledge of client performance problems with their accumulated experience with Huge's technical capabilities. There was little or no external market research. Consequently, the products were developed with the expectation that subsequent client development efforts would validate (or invalidate) individual products.

How would Huge engage new clients in discussions about their performance challenges? The company would describe the products it had for Experience Transformation, Technology Realization, and Growth Creation, and clients would respond by discussing their specific performance problems in these areas. That was the theory behind the productization approach: tee up product descriptions, and the discussion would segue quickly into deeper discussions about client performance problems. The product discussions would stimulate client responses on these more intimate and important subjects.

An alternate approach — one more commonly used by consulting firms — would potentially be considered in the future. That would call for Huge to begin discussions with potential clients by zeroing in on their performance problems. Once these were understood, the company would respond by describing the products that would solve these problems.

This other approach is certainly straightforward, and CPO De Bonis was a proponent of it. She wrote to me about the choice between product-centricity and client-centricity:

True client-centricity starts with understanding the client's context and challenges. We should be asking the Client Partnership Craft to focus on qualifying and articulating a client's biggest problems, not to have them learn and promote the ins and outs of our products. Having Client Partners take on product discussions would carry too much risk — at least for now — and should be the responsibility of the Product Pod leaders.

Baxter had other thoughts, reasoning that it would be easier for Client Partners and Product Craft executives to become fluent in describing Huge's products, rather than leading off with intimate client discussions about their performance problems. Here's what he told me about that:

The management consulting firms, like Bain, McKinsey, BCG, Kearney, and Accenture are well versed in getting senior client executives to talk openly about the problems they worry about. Consulting executives are sophisticated and trusted. Huge is not yet far enough along in its transformation to use this particular approach. It would be better and easier for us now to go the 'product first' route, and train our Client Partners and Product Craft experts to become well versed in describing our products. Discussions of performance problems by clients will come out of this as a by-product. That's what I believe, in any case, but we will not know whether or not I'm right until we've tried this out in enough situations.

Huge's product approach was similar to what was carried out at Apple under Steve Jobs, who is reported to have said:

Some people say, 'Give the customers what they want.' But that's not my approach. Our job is to figure out what they're going to want before they do. Henry Ford once said, 'If I'd asked customers what they wanted, they would have told me, a faster horse!' People don't know what they want until you show it to them. That's why I never rely on market research. Our task is to read things that are not yet on the page.[23]

People who see Jobs as an unvarnished genius, and who hope to emulate his approach for product development, should be reminded that this intuitive approach led to many product failures: Apple Lisa, NeXT, Apple III, Twentieth Anniversary Macintosh, ROKR, Power Mac G4 Cube, Puck Mouse, iTunes phone, and MobileMe. Creative inspiration is not an infallible approach, although when it creates a barn-burning winner like the iPhone, it's hard to criticize, and the associated failures, like Edison's 'one thousand light bulb failures' become something else. As Edison was reported to have said, "I didn't fail 1,000 times. The light bulb was an invention with 1,000 steps."

Philip Kotler, a professor emeritus at Northwestern University's Kellogg School of Management, and co-author of *Marketing Management*,[24] widely considered the authoritative textbook on marketing, is not enamored with the concept of pure inspiration. "Marketing," he wrote, "is the homework that we do before we have a product." Marketing inspires inspiration. It involves hard work — understanding and anticipating client needs so the products that emerge from this process can be easily sold.

By this definition, the Polpo productization team carried out marketing, even if it was principally internal marketing. It involved pooling collective experiences from the past and sharing them in a group effort that led to the creation of three doors, three performance challenges, and five drawers. The productization team might have gone further, and taken more time to conduct detailed *external* market research, with CMOs, CIOs, and CXOs, but the decision to exploit existing knowledge within Huge was thoughtful and efficient.

In any case, no one associated with the productization process would claim that the team did a perfect job defining 45 products that would solve client performance problems. It was understood by all that the real test would come over time, as efforts were made to sell the products. Feedback from the marketplace would steer the Product Pod team in adding, dropping and tweaking existing offerings, until the right mix was arrived at.

Huge's productization effort, then, was as good as it could have been. Its success — or lack of success — will be defined by the experience of actual client development efforts, along with the appropriateness of product-change tweaks by the Product Pod team.

GLOBALIZATION

Beginning in February 2022 and continuing through June 2022, Baxter unveiled the organizational transformation that would lead to phasing out the office profit center structure, turning geographical offices into experience centers, and converting Huge into a single global profit center.

The shift was a dramatic one for the organization. As one office president told me:

> *Huge is now a strategy-led organization. In the past, it was more people driven. In the past, as an office head, I was responsible for the P&L and the health and welfare of all my people. I was there to energize people culturally, to make them feel my leadership, and to create some kind of identity for them.*
>
> *That model has changed. The Client Partner role is now about the health and welfare of our clients, and about driving organic growth through our products. The management of people is handled in a different way, through the crafts and the global talent allocation system. Client Partners will serve up opportunities, and the craft leaders will execute. This model will work. It's very different, and some people, particularly those who came to Huge for what it was, might not be comfortable in the new Huge. They will leave, and this will be somewhat disruptive for a while, but eventually we will become a totally new company, and everything will stabilize around our new culture.*
>
> *I'm entirely optimistic, but we will go through some disruptions before we can call this a success.*

Baxter's all-hands announcement in September sought to reassure employees that although they were no longer bound to offices, they would each belong to a specific craft, headed by a craft leader, and they could look for continuity in their careers by virtue of the training and mentoring provided within their crafts. Client assignments would be handled thoughtfully by the Team Design and Recruiting craft in Huge's HQ. The professional opportunities afforded by a global resource allocation system would far outweigh what had existed in the past, where the number and type of clients was limited by what existed in the individual, localized offices.

POD-BASED MATRIX

As described in Chapter 9, Baxter reorganized Huge into four Client Pods, twelve Craft Pods, and three Product Pods. The members of these pods have multiple reporting relationships, and accountability is fluid, so some organizational complexities can be expected. Matrixed organizations are complicated to run, and Huge's matrix has at least three dimensions, if not more.

All company organizations have become complicated and multi-dimensional over time. In the past, organizations were made up of hierarchical units led by strong, territorial executives who controlled their operations, running them as fiefdoms. The fiefs were called strategic business units (SBUs) or decentralized profit centers, and access to their data and operations was limited to those within the units themselves. There was little transparency; SBUs were walled cities that reported their discrete financial results up to headquarters.

This changed in the 1970s with the creation of efficiency task forces, often led by engineers and procurement professionals, who invaded the SBUs and explored their operational practices. Today, it is normal for Finance, Procurement, HR, and other corporate functions to examine the workings of any organizational entity. Clients, too, participate in scrutinizing suppliers' manufacturing and marketing operations through benchmarking exercises. Management consultants, brought in for one reason or another, also roam freely through organizations to develop the data and insights they need to make their recommendations.

These developments have had the effect of reducing the absolute power of SBU leaders. 'Matrixization' is now the dominant form of organization. The number of professional executives who can leave their fingerprints on or influence SBU operations has grown significantly, creating organizational complexity. SBU leaders today must manage complicated networks of influencers. As a result, companies face collaboration challenges — figuring out how networks or groups of individuals can work effectively together. Companies design rules of engagement, like RACI systems,[25] to let the executives or specialists in a matrix organization know what roles they can play. Within a matrix, who calls the shots? Who is responsible or accountable? Who needs to be consulted or informed?

Huge has craft specialists in Creative, Strategy, Technology, Data & Insights, Client Partnership, and Program Delivery, and each of these crafts is expected to play an active role in delivering accelerated growth for clients. But what are the rules of engagement as these crafts work together in their client pods?

To address this, Huge is introducing 'job competency frameworks' to outline the required skills and job expectations for all roles in the pods. Additionally, the company is introducing an Objectives and Key Results (OKR) model so that everyone knows what outcomes they are responsible for. Additionally, a RACI model has been put in place for product delivery processes.

These accountability tools and frameworks will provide clarity and help get things done across the matrixed organization, but the systems themselves do not push the boundaries of what Huge is striving to achieve, either competitively or commercially, with its clients.

For this, Huge must rely on the axe-wielding culture that originally came into being in 1999 and continues to exist today. One of the company's great strengths, in the past and at present, is its organizational swagger: the long-standing belief that it is an exceptional company, doing exceptional client work with exceptional people. Cultures endure. The axe-wielding legacy, and the memories of the groundbreaking IKEA and JetBlue work, have given the organization an unshakeable foundation for the challenges that lie ahead.

Huge's swagger will be strengthened and reinforced by its *results mission* for its clients. And future client successes will reinforce the culture. As management guru Peter Drucker is reported to have said, "Culture eats strategy for breakfast." Strong cultures help companies endure changes in strategy and structure.

In my view, the matrix organization's complexity is unlikely to undermine Huge's mission or ability to manage itself. The company's culture will help increase its effectiveness as it takes on the challenge of improving client results. Culture, plus organizational tools like OKR and RACI, should permit the matrix organization to function effectively.

CHAPTER 12
ASSESSING PROGRESS —
THE THIRD RETREAT

Culture eats strategy for breakfast.
Credit: Dennis Flad

In October 2022, ELT members assembled in the old Brooklyn headquarters building, at 45 Main Street in Dumbo, for a three-day review of the transformation. This was the third management retreat since Baxter's appointment as CEO in June 2021.

The first retreat, in Rhode Island, in October 2021, had established the new mission — to become a growth acceleration company for the company's clients, as described in Chapter 6. This first retreat had a 'blue-sky' feel about it, asking what it takes to become a great company, as a way of confronting the past and establishing a forward-looking mission.

A second retreat, in Connecticut, in May of 2022, had dealt with a nuts-and-bolts review of the progress of the various work streams of the transformation. There were progress reports on the new operating system; client partner training; product design efforts; team resourcing methodologies; the website rewrite; the organizational design concept; new business growth planning; real estate strategy; workplace employee issues; and Huge's reputation management. TBMC had been working on many of these topics with the team since September 2021, so the various workstreams had been in running for eight months.

The third retreat was more reflective than the previous retreats. The pace of transformation change had slowed, and the mission, products, organization, and processes were in place, even though major tweaks were certainly expected. The new concept and organization had been communicated to employees, and offices were closed, at least conceptually, becoming experience centers that hosted events and gatherings of one type or another. Employees no longer reported to their previous office heads. Instead, they reported to their craft heads, and most employees were already working on clients, and they would eventually be part of a global pool of resources for future client assignments.

Baxter's planning for the third retreat followed his usual pattern. He did not discuss his overall agendas in advance. The schedule for the first day of the retreats was revealed only when ELT members arrived for a pre-meeting breakfast. The agendas for the remaining days of each retreat followed the usual pattern — they were published early on the day. This gave Baxter flexibility to adjust the agendas for the second and third days. His usual practice was to give a 15-minute speech at the beginning of each day, and then follow the format and timing of the day's agenda, adjusting the timings as required.

Consequently, ELT participants did not have any advanced insights into the overall purpose of the retreat, even though individual members might be asked to prepare presentations on one subject or another.

For the third retreat, Tess Bricker sent each attendee a blank 'Fears — Gaps — Challenges' template in advance. It was to be filled in and submitted before the third and final day of the retreat. The format was simple: on one chart, each executive was asked to identify one fear, one gap, and one challenge facing the company. Each would be given five minutes on the final day to show his or her slide and describe its content. This process would take two hours, and the 23 ELT attendees (up from 20 at the first retreat due to an increase in ELT membership) would then have the opportunity to discuss their concerns as a group.

Despite the planned schedule, the discussion of Fears, Gaps, and Challenges could not wait until the final day of the retreat. The shape and character of the transformed Huge was top-of-mind for ELT members, and they were itching to talk about it with one another.

The proposed first day's agenda for the third retreat was a modest one. Baxter would make some opening remarks. These would be followed by a one-hour discussion of financial planning for 2022 and 2023, followed by a 90-minute presentation on new business and marketing strategies. In the afternoon, participants would hear an update on DE&I progress, followed by a presentation on how the Client Pods and Craft Pods might operate as organizations that, within the pods, would be accountable for various decisions and activity. The day would conclude with a 45-minute general discussion period.

Baxter opened the meeting with a ten-minute introduction:

We have a packed agenda. Today, we'll have an informal update about what is going on in the business. We're going to go through our new marketing strategy. We'll hear a DE&I update from Toni Lowe. We have some information about how the pods are going to work. Today will be an information day. Tomorrow and the third day will be much more open for discussions, so we'll want you to be prepared to throw your opinions and your thinking at us.

Reacting to comments about productization, Baxter clarified that it was not an off-the-shelf, cookie-cutter strategy:

We sold some products in the past few months, and there was an expectation amongst some of our people that they would have everything given to them — everything that would be needed for our clients. Off-the-shelf products.

That is not the way our products were designed. Products were designed to guide our direction with quality control, creative input, and standards about how to get to our destinations. We cannot over-value or be confused about our product strategy. Our product strategy is a way of wrapping up our services. The products are roads that we built. They're really good quality roads, with no potholes, and they take you to predefined destinations — that's what the products do. The products don't do the work for you and then magically deliver results. We never designed our products to work that way. Our products are roadways to destinations, not off-the-shelf deliverables that we sell to our clients. We are still in a creative delivery business. Our journey remains a creative one.

Baxter paused at this point and asked a question: "Does anyone have anything that they think is a burning issue?"

One executive accepted this invitation:

I think we should address the culture and the work. I think it's very important to know how we can create an exciting culture in spite of remote working, one where our employees can continue to do the best work of their lives, whether or not they are going to offices to work.

Another attendee picked up the thread:

We talk about going from being a service provider to becoming a performance partner for our clients. How do we empower our people to make this transition? How do we train them, and how do we put our people in a position to work confidently on performance problems? We need to get to a place where everyone feels confident and empowered to play this new role.

The conversation picked up steam as others jumped in. Someone asked how they were to go about strengthening the culture that was required for the transformation:

How do we train our people in a remote world? How do we harness what we benefited from when we were growing up in this industry? I'd hate to see our junior people sitting in their apartments, not having the benefit of listening and learning and watching the performance of our senior leaders. Any gaps in mentoring due to remote working may come back to haunt us in two to three years. We've inherited a remote culture due to Covid. We have to find a way to overcome the weaknesses that this might create.

Another expressed concern about recruiting and retaining talent in a global, flexible-working environment:

We will need even more world-class talent in the future. We have the challenge of developing a client-centric brand out of our client service model, and doing it while so many of our employees are working remotely.

One participant summarized the current situation at Huge:

We shouldn't be surprised by our concerns. We've been engaged for the last year in changing our company, and this came at a very tough time because of Covid. That's what we've been doing. And even though everyone around this table has been planning and implementing great and positive things for the transformation, the sum of these things has not created a new culture. What matters is what we have not yet done. We have not mobilized our new set of things — our mission, our productization, our globalization, our new organization — to create a new culture for our employees. It's much too early. We've talked about it with one another, and we believe in it, but the new culture will not be in place until we have been operational for some time. Our people are aware of what we have changed. They have not experienced what we want to become.

So, why are we surprised that it's confusing right now?

We have a new job ahead of us. Let's sit down and create the new Huge culture as fast as we can. We've done a great thing in two dimensions. We got rid of the old and we created the basis for the new. It's a great story, but we're not done.

We need to start on creating a new Huge culture. We have to overcome the constraints of remote working. We have to create a new, meaningful culture that ties our organization together.

The group plowed through the opening day's agenda, leaving these first-morning concerns to be dealt with on the second and third day. Baxter adjusted the second day's agenda so that the Client Pod Presidents could show their colleagues how they were dealing with each of the clients in their portfolios. They'd lay out how they were mobilizing their matrixed organizations to work effectively, bringing multidisciplinary resources, craft by craft, into their client operations, using the accountability frameworks. They discussed their existing clients and the prospects for growth for the last quarter of 2022, and revealed their ambitions and challenges for 2023.

The Client Pod presentations reduced the stress of the first day's discussion and led to dialogue about client-centricity — a relief for those who felt that day one was too focused on internal issues caused by remote working.

Finally, on the third day, the group turned its attention to the Fears, Gaps, and Challenges. Baxter could not attend this particular session, but would join later, via Zoom, for the final wrap-up.

Attendees seemed nonplussed by his absence. By now, the team members were a tight group, used to dealing with one another in a collaborative way. I had been observing the ELT's workings for the past year, and one of its great strengths was a lack of personal gossip, overt ambition, or behind-the-scenes backbiting. As a group, team members seemed to accept one another as equals, each working on a different piece of the puzzle. For the past year, the team worked without friction, without gripes about one another, or complaints about the direction things were moving.

CPO De Bonis hosted the two-hour Fears, Gaps, and Challenges discussion, holding participants to five minutes each to keep things from getting bogged down by deep dives into one concern or another.

The Fears were expressed through words like attrition; organizational paralysis; lost faith; missing talent; revenue shortfalls; staffing challenges; slowing heartbeat; losing talent; loss of trust; poor information; messy systems; silo creation; and unclear roles.

The Gaps were characterized as the ability to explain change; prioritization of training; lack of emerging leaders; lack of fun; tech shortfalls; lack of international growth; too much complexity; lack of diversity; loose leadership; and insufficient focus on creativity.

The Challenges were described as living in the old and new worlds at the same time; increasing a sense of urgency; creating a new Huge brand; learning how to give work-focused feedback; learning how to slow down; filling talent gaps; becoming client-centric; recruiting; growing internationally; improving morale; dealing with remote working; and improving the quality of work.

Ironically, given the intensity of concerns that were expressed on the first day, the Fears, Gaps, and Challenges review had a business-as-usual feel about it. The concerns sounded like what any well-meaning group of executives might offer up, in virtually any sort of company.

Something had changed over the three days. The Fears, Gaps, and Challenges created a list of issues that felt manageable. There were issues to be dealt with, to be sure, but they were well within the capabilities of the ELT members, who went through them with a degree of confidence.

As De Bonis drew the discussion to a close, the executives looked around the room and grinned at each other, as if to say, 'Hey, that wasn't so bad!' I saw some participants high-fiving one another. It was if they had given it their worst — digging deep to express their most profound worries — and failed to frighten themselves.

Instead, the exercise was a victory of sorts. It said, 'We can handle whatever comes our way.'

––––––––––––

Baxter joined the group via Zoom for the retreat's wrap-up, offering this perspective:

I would like to thank all of you for what you accomplished over three days. We are better leaders when we challenge each other. We are better leaders when we bring issues to the table, not just pat each other on the back and say how legendary we are. I have been in plenty of leadership groups where that is the dynamic. Instead, there were some really hard conversations over the last three days, but they were in the right spirit.

The conversations were in the spirit of making the company better, making our people and our culture better, and making us as a leadership team better. And that's what we are here to do. It can feel overwhelming for three days to sit and do what this group does, which is to self-analyze and criticize its own actions and its own performance in a way that only a high-performance group can. That's the real danger when you get a bunch of high-performing people together — everyone's self-critical, leaving you with the belief that the whole thing is running off the rails.

There are many things going on here that worry me and make me nervous. And do you know what? I reflected on them last night and I reframed them in my head. The fact is we all sat around and did what we did, and got a grasp of all of the things that we know we have to get better at.

That is great leadership. That is us running the company properly. And so, I want us to come away from these last three days feeling as though we have done our job as leaders, and that we have not fallen into an internal echo chamber of how great we are and how great everything is. It is not all great, and it should not be. We're a year into a radical transformation. We are taking the company into a different and new place. It is not all going be perfect and brilliant, and we are not all amazing, like the gymnast who springs off the beam and lands perfectly.

We are not always going to do that. We are going to stumble. We are going to fall over occasionally. But we will pick ourselves up, dust ourselves off, and do a better job next time. And one day, we will all spring off the beam and land perfectly.

CHAPTER 13
PROGRESS

*"You must keep your foot on the accelerator, flat to the floor,
and avoid the temptation to back off, even when things get
a little wobbly and you're approaching a curve in the road."*

Credit: Dennis Flad

One week after the retreat, Baxter called me with some good news. Huge had won three major new clients, selling them relationships and products that added up to millions of dollars in new sales. The Product Pod worked hand-in-hand with the global Client Pods to develop the sales proposals and convert the business. The pod executives did the selling; Baxter was not personally involved. Here's what that told him:

> *I always knew that we had the potential to give our clients what they really need, which is topline growth. In all three of these cases, we were speaking the same language as our clients, and we sold them products that address their specific growth challenges.*
>
> *If we had been going about client development as we had in the past, we would never have had this kind of success.*
>
> *I'm buoyed by this confirmation that our new mission and our products work in the marketplace. This is just the beginning, but it is a beginning — we need to overcome some of the organizational issues that we identified at the retreat last week.*

Given all the concerns about winning over new employees, operating on a global basis, running a complicated organization, and creating a new culture, did Baxter he feel that the ELT made progress in addressing these issues? Was he happy with the result?

> *I'm quite confident that we created the right solution for ourselves. We have a new mission, a suite of powerful products, a global structure, and a new form of pod organization. The amount of change has been staggering. We had no choice about this. We had to go very far and very fast to get to a new place, and although we have not solved everything we face, we eventually will. We're already in a much better place.*
>
> *Being a 180 mile-per-hour business simply will not cut it. Our ambition is to be a 200 mile-per-hour, high-performance company. And in order to achieve that sort of performance, you have to believe in the integrity and quality of the vehicle you have designed and are driving. You must have the courage to keep your foot on the accelerator, flat to the floor, and avoid the temptation to back off, even when things get a little wobbly and you're approaching a curve in the road.*
>
> *You cannot flinch, not even for an instant. Instead, you have to believe that you will not crash the car — that you, and the car, can handle the conditions.*
>
> *That's how you reach 200 miles-per-hour, and that's how you truly transform a company.*

CHAPTER 14
PARADIGM SHIFT

"Welcome to the Paradigm Shift!"
Credit: Dennis Flad

The failure of existing rules is the prelude to a search for new ones.
—Thomas S. Kuhn

Despite the evidence of progress by the end of 2022, it is too early — and certainly unrealistic — to judge Huge's transformation based on improved results from sales of new products or the functioning of its new organization.

Its transformation has to be viewed as more than the creation of performance-fixing products, the design of a pod-based organization, or getting senior executives to engage in a corporate transformation project. Huge did of course accomplish these things, and they were done with intensity, enthusiasm, and commitment, driven by Baxter's leadership and energy. And we are understandably interested in how well the transformation will help deliver accelerated growth for clients, more meaningful employment experiences for the company's global workforce, and improved financial results for Huge and IPG. However, it is too early to know how well the transformation will work along these dimensions.

The transformation is greater than the sum its actions, and we would be wrong to judge it based solely on the results it generates in the near term.

Instead, we need to view the transformation in a larger sense — as a paradigm shift in a changing industry, offering a new template for executives to exploit in unique ways, to set new directions for themselves.

What do we mean by the now rather dated sounding term *paradigm shift*? It's lost much of its original meaning since physicist and philosopher Thomas Kuhn introduced it in his seminal 1962 book, *The Structure of Scientific Revolutions*.[26] This is unfortunate. The term is now used to describe very ordinary changes.[27] Kuhn — who examined how science and scientists evolve in the face of new data and learning — used "paradigm change" to describe dramatic changes in the theory and practice of science.

In its original context, Kuhn wrote about a revolutionary change in the direction of science, based on the articulation of new theories that better explain the outcomes from scientific observations and experimentation. Examples abound: Copernicus (1543) articulated a paradigm shift by putting the sun at the center of the universe, challenging the traditional Ptolemaic paradigm that saw the Earth at its center. Henceforth, mathematical calculations about planetary movements using the Copernicus paradigm could proceed on a different basis. Copernicus' theory shifted the paradigm about the structure of the universe and the planets' movements through space. This was not a minor paradigm shift, given the strength of the Roman Catholic dogma that the Earth's divine creation put it at the center of the universe. The philosopher Giordano Bruno was burned at the stake in 1600 over his refusal to recant his belief in Copernicus' heliocentric paradigm.

Einstein's theories of special relativity (1905) and general relativity (1915) replaced the simpler Newtonian concepts of gravity, mass, and time. The Einsteinian paradigms have fueled decades of groundbreaking scientific data gathering and research that could not be carried out if scientists relied on the Newtonian paradigm. Einstein's paradigms are validated over and over again through scientific research and discovery. For instance, research published in the journal *Physical Review X* in 2021 challenged several of Einstein's predictions by observing a double-pulsar star system around 2,400 light-years from Earth. Indeed, each of the seven predictions of general relativity was confirmed by the study.[28]

Science advances in fits and starts by going through a process that involves: 1) normal scientific investigations under the umbrella of existing paradigms; 2) crises, when experimental data diverge significantly from the expectations of existing paradigms; 3) paradigm change, when new theories better explain the data, setting new directions for experimentation; and then 4) new scientific investigations, involving experiments based on new paradigms.

Over long periods of time, science lurches from stability to crisis to stability again. Bear in mind, crises, as Kuhn defines them, occur when data from experimentation diverge significantly from what the existing theories predict. Scientific revolutions occur when new theories do a better job of explaining actual outcomes. They replace old theories, and scientific experimentation moves in new directions. Paradigm shifts are generated by new theories.

What does this have to do with advertising and developments in the ad industry?

Advertising, like science, operates under an existing paradigm — a theory of advertising — and a very specific paradigm has been in place since about 1960. Let's call this the creative paradigm. It holds that advertising is about creativity, which is required to generate improved results for clients. Bill Bernbach, George Lois, and Leo Burnett are seen as the great inventors and proponents of this paradigm, which turned advertising on its head during the Creative Revolution of the 1960s, leading to the creation of groundbreaking ads like those shown here:

The man in the Hathaway shirt

Lemon.

Avis is only No.2
in rent a cars.
So why go with us?

We try harder.
(When you're not the biggest, you have to.)
We just can't afford dirty ashtrays. Or half-empty
gas tanks. Or worn wipers. Or unwashed cars. Or low
tires. Or anything less than seat-adjusters that adjust.
Heaters that heat. Defrosters that defrost.
Obviously, the thing we try hardest for is just to be
nice. To start you out right with a new car, like a lively,
super-torque Ford, and a pleasant smile. To know, say,
where you get a good pastrami sandwich in Duluth.
Why?
Because we can't afford to take you for granted.
Go with us next time.
The line at our counter is shorter.

Since the Creative Revolution, ad agency employees and clients have been told that creativity is the principal source of success in the industry — for the winning of new clients, the creation of successful brands, the generation of attractive levels of compensation, and the maintenance of competitive success for agencies. During the internet age, creativity was joined by data analysis to create this success, but creativity is still seen as the driver. Creative awards have been invented to acknowledge the centrality of creativity for the industry. The CEO of one major ad agency appends the following signature to all of his emails:

- Most Effective Network in the World, 2011, 2014, 2015, 2017, 2020 Global Effie Index
- Network of the Decade, 2021 Cannes Festival of Creativity
- Network of the Year, Cannes Festival, 2007, 2008, 2009, 2010, 2011, 2017, 2018
- Network of the Year, World Advertising Research Center, 2006, 2007, 2008, 2009, 2010, 2011, 2012, 2013, 2014, 2015, 2016, 2017, 2018, 2019
- Network of the Year, The Big Won Report as Most Creative Network Across All Communications Platforms, 2007, 2008, 2009, 2010, 2011, 2012, 2014, 2015, 2016, 2018

- Global Network of the Year, Adweek Magazine, 2011, 2014
- Network of the Year, Campaign Magazine, 2005, 2007, 2008, 2011, 2015, 2017
- Most Strategic Network in the World, WARC 100, 2014, 2015, 2016, 2017, 2018
- WARC "Best of the Best" network, 2019

The creative paradigm has provided the theoretical underpinning for the practice of advertising for the past 60 years.

What this does not explain, though, is that for many decades, the *business* of advertising has not met the expectations of *this theory* of advertising, as I described in *Madison Avenue Manslaughter*. This suggests the need for a new paradigm.

What are the gaps between theory and outcomes? What is the basis for questioning the creative paradigm?

1. **Moribund growth rates for advertisers.** Since 2009, advertiser growth has been quite low, despite major creative investments in digital and social media. Between 2009 (post-financial meltdown) and 2019 (pre-Covid), major advertisers underperformed in sales growth, and a high percentage of the top 50 advertisers actually declined in topline sales.[29] The creative paradigm has not generated consistently healthy sales performance for advertisers. This suggests that agency creativity is not enough. Something more is needed.

2. **Declining prices for agency work.** Pure creativity is not being rewarded by clients. Award-winning agencies are paid no better than 'ordinary' ones. Prices for agency creative work have been declining regularly, by up to 4.5% per year, and are now only a third of the prices enjoyed 30 years ago. The creative paradigm assumes that creativity is valuable and should provide the basis for business and financial success. This is not the case today. Something more is needed.

3. **Turnover of agency relationships.** Agency relationships with clients, which used to last 20-plus years, now last only three years or so, and the industry is marked by constant changes of CMOs and

subsequent firings and hirings of agencies. Indeed, the turnover of agency relationships is so prevalent that senior agency executives have to focus heavily on winning new clients to replace those they've lost for one reason or another. Creativity is not generating stability in the industry. Something more is needed.

4. **Talent issues.** Agencies used to hire the best Ivy-League graduates, turn them into creatives or account executives, pay them exceptionally well, and watch their careers grow. Today, many of those kinds of graduates go to consulting firms and Wall Street banks. Agencies are finding it more difficult to hire and keep the most talented graduates; starting salaries are 40–50% below what the consulting firms and Wall Street offer. The creative paradigm is not creating a business environment that attracts and keeps the best talent for agency needs. Something more is needed.

Kuhn noted that scientists will continue to go down familiar, well-trodden paths until someone — usually a young outsider — articulates a new paradigm. Science depends on new paradigms to nourish itself and sustain its ongoing revolutions. Here's how Kuhn characterized the push and pull of paradigm change:

> *Almost always the men who achieve these fundamental inventions of a new paradigm have been either very young or very new to the field whose paradigm they change... these are the men who, being little committed by prior practice to the traditional rules of normal science, are particularly likely to see that those rules no longer define a playable game, and they conceive others that can replace them.*[30]

When Baxter arrived at Huge, having worked entirely within media agencies, rather than creative shops, he proposed continued investments in creative thinking *plus* the 'something more is needed' element noted above. What was this missing ingredient? A single-minded focus on organizing to achieve improved client results.

This is evident from the dialogue he led at that first executive retreat, as outlined in Chapter 6. Baxter did not abandon creativity as an essential ingredient in Huge's work. Quite the opposite.

He focused on *outcomes* rather than on internal capabilities. He made it clear that improved client results had to provide the basis for the company's mission and the measure of its success, and that all of Huge's capabilities had to be focused on this end. Later, once the transformation elements were in place, it was clear that creativity needed to be mobilized — with specialized products and highly skilled, collaborative teams — to bring about improved client results.

In effect, this was proposing a *results paradigm* for Huge. The ELT embraced the concept wholeheartedly.

Huge's results paradigm includes: 1) a corporate mission to improve client results; 2) an understanding of the key performance problems facing clients; 3) a joint commitment by the client and Huge to solve these problems together; 4) a suite of products designed to solve client problems; 5) product-based pricing; 6) appropriate strategic, creative, technical, analytical and delivery resources; and 7) an organizational structure and processes to allocate these resources to products and clients for problem-solving purposes.

A results paradigm is not a new thing in business, but it is new to the advertising industry. Management consultants have long embraced the approach. Bain & Company was founded in 1973 on the principle that consultants must measure their success in terms of their clients' improved financial results. To that end, for nearly 50 years Bain has published analyses that show that its clients have outperformed the stock market by 4 to 1.

Baxter's achievements involved: 1) articulating an outcomes-focused results paradigm for Huge; 2) following through with the creation of new products; and 3) putting in place an innovative global structure that helps deliver on the client-results promise.

The articulation of the new results paradigm set Huge off in new directions. And, inevitably, new directions create new issues and problems. New paradigms do not, in and of themselves, solve all the problems associated with the previous paradigm. As Kuhn pointed out, "[We should] remember what a paradigm debate is about. When a new candidate for paradigm is first proposed, it has seldom solved more than a few of the problems that confront it, and most of those solutions are still far from perfect."[31]

A new paradigm sets new directions, and new issues will be encountered along the way, even long after the paradigm has first been embraced. Huge's results may suffer as it attempts to wind down the old and implement the new. The company may lose employees who find its transition personally uncomfortable. It may encounter some initial difficulties in selling its new, reinvented products to clients. Other issues will likely present themselves along the way, as Huge's results paradigm is being implemented.

However, the issues that arise can be dealt with. It will simply take some time for the results paradigm to become bedded down and running smoothly.

Baxter's leadership team seems ready for this challenge — the third management retreat showed their mettle.

The results paradigm provides a new template for the industry. It is by no means an abandonment of creativity. Instead, the new approach puts creativity, products, and organization together in a focused mission.

Others who embrace the results paradigm may make different choices, based on who they are and what they do. Huge's specific products and organizational design are *details and choices* that reflect the company's view of its needs. Other agencies may elect to create different products and organizational structures.

What is clear is that the advertising industry now has a results paradigm to consider. We can hope that this prospect will lead to renewed creative effectiveness for the benefit of clients, renewed financial health for agencies, and renewed employee satisfaction among those who work in the industry.

APPENDIX
HUGE'S REORGANIZATION: FAQS

PREPARED AND DISTRIBUTED BY HUGE'S EXECUTIVE LEADERSHIP TEAM

On the following pages we hope to answer many of your most pressing questions regarding our new organizational structure.

We acknowledge that this transformation is new, ambitious, and may be a little audacious. Like all Huge moves, it will require ongoing optimization and iteration, which means we are all going to be learning a lot together. We will be updating the FAQs when new questions and answers emerge.

We also invite questions and feedback throughout this journey.

THE REORG ITSELF

Q: What are the biggest organizational challenges we are solving with this reorganization?

The most inspiring mission in the world will fail if the structure to deliver it is flawed, inconsistent, or lacking. Our old structure as it existed before did not allow for us to realize our ambition to become a creative growth accelerator. It was rigid, outdated, and out of alignment with our new business strategy. It was simply an inferior design for our lofty ambitions.

For much of our 20-plus years, Huge was organized as a collection of offices, operating independently under the Huge brand. At one point in time, the concept of offices made sense, but that model is no longer scalable or relevant in the world we operate in now. Post-pandemic, amid our fully flexible work environment, the regional office structure had become a detriment to our growth. Our offices sometimes operated in conflict with one another — selfishly gatekeeping opportunities, limiting the growth of our business and of our people, and limiting our ability to innovate on behalf of clients and ourselves.

A good organizational structure should help us do the best work of our lives, without the old frictions. It should advance our commercial model and our employee value proposition. It should facilitate business growth and people growth. Getting there required us to make a huge move of our own.

Q: What is the objective of the reorganization?

Its primary objective is to create one globally-connected company. By aligning under a new, cohesive structure, we can realize our business ambitions while helping our people realize their career ambitions.

The reorganization is more than a realignment of teams. It is our collective commitment to an entirely new way of working, and a recognition of our need to accelerate the changes we need to achieve our goals.

Specifically, our new structure was designed to:

- Enable Huge to stand out in a crowded and competitive market
- Elevate the nature and value of our client relationships
- Increase the quality, speed, and value of what we sell and how we deliver it
- Improve the depth of diversity, expertise, and excellence in our crafts
- Decrease the amount of time spent recreating the same processes over and over (and over) again
- Make us a much more successful company

Q: What was the guiding principle of the reorganization?

Throughout this entire process, our guiding principle has been to create as little disruption as possible, while still accelerating our people and business growth. Our reorganization was done with extreme sensitivity towards client dynamics and an appreciation for relationships, both client-side and internal. We feel confident that we have achieved our goal here.

Q: What are the core elements of the reorganization?

The reorganization represents our desire to be:

- Client-centric
- Product-oriented
- Craft-powered

To that end, we have realigned ourselves globally into three Pod types. The first is our Client Pods, which are central to the new organizational structure. This is where client relationships will be nurtured and grown. Client Pods are the home bases for the crafts of Client Partnership and Program Delivery.

Then there are our Craft Pods. These will provide depth and breadth of expertise across strategy, data & insights, creative, and technology. Given the capacity of those four crafts, globally, this will be the new home base for 60% of our talent around the world.

The Craft Pods will also be organized around a brand new concept we are introducing, called Craft Communities. These groups will enable deeper development of specific skills, more focused collaboration and team development, and the creation of reputation-generating thought leadership. Craft Communities will bring together a specialized group of people who share a passion for what they do. They are designed to be a safe environment in which to explore and push the boundaries of our crafts together. The term 'community' reflects a lack of rigidity, and sets the foundation for fluidity, openness and cross-training.

The new pod structure will enable us to better:

- Leverage our skills as a global company
- Meet client needs
- Deliver efficiencies
- Achieve true interoperability and cross-collaboration

Third, as we have shared, Huge will go to market with a bold new product strategy. Our new products will help unlock greater speed, consistency and quality in our work, thus increasing its overall value. This initiative is being led by our Product Pods, which will help our Client Pod teams sell new products and provide specialist guidance to other teams.

Huge HQ will include the crafts of DE&I, growth, talent, finance, legal and operations.

THE CLIENT PODS

Q: How many Client Pods will we have at Huge?

We will have four Global Client Pods.

Q: Who will lead each of the four Client Pods, and what are they called?

Each Client Pod will be led by a president, along with a lean, cross-craft leadership team consisting of a client partner lead, an operations lead, a program delivery lead, a strategy lead, a creative lead, and a technology lead. The four presidents are:

- Jon Judah, Client Pod 10
- Matt Weiss, Client Pod 72
- Blake Wirht, Client Pod 99
- Alex Pym, Client Pod 05

Client Pod presidents and their cross-craft leadership teams will be accountable for the health and growth of their respective client portfolios. Their remit is to build deep, trust-based relationships with senior-level clients, and be looked on as experts in their businesses and industries, and in turn increase the value of our engagements, year over year. This evolution in our leadership structure will allow for greater visibility into our clients' marketplaces, and grant us a more accurate view of their priorities, challenges, and untapped opportunities.

Q: Will the cross-craft leadership team in the Client Pods work with clients?

Yes, absolutely. Each member of the cross-craft leadership team will be broadly accountable for ALL clients in their respective Client Pod, but each will also get deeply involved on at least one global Top 50 client, to realize outcomes for our client and to help drive retention and growth of that client relationship for Huge.

Q: How will the Client Pods be structured?

Client Pod teams are central to our mission. This is where the work happens — where everyone comes together to think, collaborate and do the best work of their lives. The Client Pods will keep everyone focused on the clients and their needs, to ensure they are positioned at the heart of everything we do.

Each Client Pod will have a broad portfolio of clients, other than CP99, which collaborates exclusively with a single, long-standing global partner. Every Client Pod president will be supported by a cross-craft leadership team consisting of a client partner lead, an operations lead, a program delivery lead, a strategy lead, a creative lead, and a technology lead.

Client Partnership and Program Management are crafts that will be structured within the Client Pods, given the critical roles they play in building long-term partnership with clients and delivering work for clients. The Client Partnership team reports to Matt Di Paola (Chief Client Partner) and the Program Delivery team reports to Mark Manning (Chief Operating Officer).

Q: If I work on client projects, am I automatically in a Client Pod?

No. Simply working on a client project or retainer that lives within a specific Client Pod portfolio does not make you a member of that Client Pod. If your craft is Client Partnership or Program Delivery, or if you are a member of a Client Pod leadership team, then yes, you are officially in a Client Pod. But if you represent another craft, such as strategy, creative, technology, or data & insights, then you do not. This is an important distinction: while members of the Craft Pod work on client projects and are part of a client team, they are not members of the Client Pod. If they were, then our Client Pods would just be 'offices' with another name. If you are a member of the Craft Pod, over time you should expect to work across several Client Pods — and most importantly, on several clients — as your skills are matched with client needs across the company. By creating a much more porous structure between Client and Craft Pod, it is our intention to break down the silos that previously existed between offices and regions.

Q: What is happening to the role of regional presidents?

Regional presidents have shifted into leadership roles in both our Client and Craft Pods.

Q: What happened to the offices and the regions?

Over the past year, we have already started the transition into a 100% flexible workforce, and we are now embarking on a more sweeping change, which will shift us away from our former, regional-based model.

Part of this transformation entails realigning what people traditionally thought to be their home base. Instead of by region or office, employees will now be grouped by globally aligned crafts and by the clients that they work on.

This does not mean people move out of the area they have called home, and it does not mean that we're completely doing away with all of our physical offices. In fact, we recently announced a major investment in a Brooklyn-based Experience Centre, located in the Brooklyn Navy Yard. But it does, however, mean that as an organization, we can now redeploy our hiring efforts to reach beyond our old, geographically defined talent pools, and it means that individuals have the freedom to work on great projects without being constrained only by client projects within their region's geographic location.

Q: Why do the Client Pods have such simple names?

We have kept the names simple intentionally. This supports our focus on being One Huge, client-centric and people-centric. Each Client Pod name honors a milestone in Huge's history.

- CP99 - The founding
- CP05 - The axe
- CP10 - The Goat
- CP72 - The Navy Yard

Q: Will moving to Client Pods reduce operational problems?

Yes. Our new, more integrated structure is an important step in reducing operational friction. The pod structure, complemented by the other elements of our transformation, is intended to enable increased collaboration, streamlined processes and the leveraging of our full, global capabilities. These are key elements of a stronger operation.

Q: How were the Client Pods determined? Are they based on more than regional considerations?

Client Pods were determined by industry expertise and our desire to minimize disruptions to existing tracks of work. We also factored in the size of each portfolio and make-up of clients to ensure equity in size and opportunity between portfolios. Finally, we transitioned some clients into new portfolios based on where the teams were best suited to support the client teams, provide value to the clients, and grow those clients and Huge's business longer term.

Q: For a net new business opportunity, how will we decide which Client Pod takes the initiative?

Under our new organizational structure, new business opportunities can be more equitably shared across the Client Pods. This is because, unlike offices, Client Pods are not constrained by limited talent resources or expertise. Under the new model, anyone in the Craft Pod can support any Client Pod as needed, and as a result any Client Pod can meet (and surpass) the needs of any client. The Growth craft will work directly with our new clients and the Client Pod leadership teams to determine the best fit for each opportunity. Sometimes it may be based on which Client Pod has the right resource profile in close proximity to the client's headquarters. Other times, it will be based on vacancy within a Client Pod's portfolio, work-type expertise, relationships, chemistry, industry expertise, areas of interest, or the desire to manage a perceived conflict.

Q: One of the benefits of the regions was that they provided some distance between clients. How will we manage potential or perceived conflicts now?

Client relationships are still organized and managed within Client Pods to mitigate any potential or perceived conflicts, and to maintain and nurture client relationships.

Q: Offices and regions were an important source of Huge's culture. How will we compensate for that now that they no longer exist in the company's new structure?

Each Client Pod, Craft Pod, and Craft Community will be responsible for creating new rituals and experiences to foster growth, collaboration and camaraderie, throughout the company and across the various talent hubs.

Q: Can people work across multiple Client Pods?

If your craft is structured within the Craft Pod (i.e., Strategy, Creative, Data & Insights, Technology), you should anticipate working across Client Pods — and, importantly, across a variety of clients whose needs match your skills. If your craft is structured within the Client Pod (i.e., Client Partnership and Program Delivery), you will primarily work with clients that fall within the Client Pod to which you're assigned. Over time, however, you will have opportunities to work with clients in other Client Pods as well.

Q: Why did we rename Program Management to Program Delivery?

It was done to clarify the craft's role in the organization and to better signal the value of the craft to our clients. As a global craft, Program Management is the craft accountable for delivery. The new Program Delivery name allows us to signal this accountability more clearly to colleagues at Huge, and to our clients as well. This is not a craft focused on the passive 'management' of programs of work. It is a craft proactively focused on the efficient and effective delivery of programs and projects for our clients.

THE CRAFT PODS

Q: What are the crafts specifically within the Craft Pods?

- Creative
- Strategy
- Technology
- Data & Insights

Client Partnership and Program Delivery are crafts structured within the Client Pods.

DE&I, Growth, Operations, Talent, Finance, and Legal are crafts structured within Huge HQ.

Q: Who are the leaders for all our global crafts, including the crafts in the Craft Pod?

- Creative: Fura Johannesdottir
- Strategy: Ryan Ku
- Technology: Brian Fletcher
- Data & Insights: Frisco Chau
- Growth: Alex Pym
- DE&I: Toni Lowe
- Program Delivery: Mark Manning
- Talent: Adrienne Imbriaco
- Team Design: Mimi Moore
- Operations: Mark Manning
- Finance: Urvashi Shivdasani
- Legal: Chris Wlach
- Client Partnership: Matt Di Paola

Global Craft leaders are responsible for establishing vibrant, diverse global Craft Communities and growing our talent within each respective craft. These individuals are constantly looking across the network at the skills we have, and assessing those we will need in the future, to consistently deliver the highest quality work, and staff the highest quality talent.

Q: What is a Craft Community?

Certain Crafts will be organized around a brand new construct we are introducing, called Craft Communities. These can be viewed as specific capabilities within each Craft Pod. Communities create a dedicated space to go deeper into the development of specific specialized skills, as well as more focused collaboration, team development, and the more efficient creation of reputation-generating thought leadership.

Q: How were the Craft Communities determined?

They were determined after a thorough analysis of our clients' needs, market trends, and the competitive landscape. We believe that our Craft Communities represent the right skills and passions we need to become a growth accelerator for our clients, by increasing their creative capital.

Q: What are Craft Community leads?

Each Craft Community has a leader. These individuals will be accountable for being exceptional at their specialized craft, multipliers of capability, and developers of people. They are also accountable to have the business acumen to leverage their strengths to meet our organizational goals.

Q: Will Craft Community leads get to work with clients?

Absolutely. Craft Community leads will bring their senior-level craft leadership to one critical Top 50 global client relationship, to drive outcomes for our client and to help drive retention and growth of that relationship for Huge.

Q: Why do some crafts not have Craft Communities?

All crafts have Craft Communities, but some crafts by their very nature require deeper development of areas of expertise and more specialized skills development, which is where smaller Craft Communities become important. For example, Technology has 300 people in the craft, and breaking that large global group into smaller, manageable Craft Communities provides a better community for our people in that craft. For other crafts —

like Program Delivery, where the required expertise is expected to be more consistent and generalized across the organization — the entire craft can be considered one large Craft Community. Regardless of whether your respective craft has one large Craft Community or a few specialized Craft Communities, Global Craft leaders will be expected to support all members of their respective crafts with clear expectations, the development of new skills, and the establishment of a global culture and community through forums, new rituals, and shared best practices across the company.

Q: Why is Studio not listed as a Craft Community?

Studio is part of the Creative craft (and structured within the Craft Pod), but as a capability it will be leveraged by the Client Pod for client work and Huge HQ for internal growth initiatives. It continues to be led by Kim Cortese. In addition to leading Studio, Cortese is a member of the global Creative leadership team.

Q: Will Craft Community members work directly with clients? Will they lead client engagements?

Yes, and yes. An individual's Craft Community alignment has no bearing on the individual's current project assignments, so if someone is currently working directly with clients, they will continue to do so. Opportunities to lead a client engagement will be open to anyone who has the needed capabilities and experience, regardless of their Craft Community alignment.

Q: Will Craft Community members work on new business?

Individuals will have the opportunity, and be invited, to work on specific product sales or other new business initiatives whenever their expertise or experience is needed.

Q: Why was I aligned to a particular Craft Community?

Craft Community alignment was informed by an individual's specific expertise, experience, and skills. Individuals were selected for a particular craft community based on what they could learn, as well as what they could contribute.

**Q: Can someone switch Craft Communities?
What is the process?**

Alignment to Craft Communities was thoughtful, based on an understanding of an individual's skills and expertise and how those align to the Craft Community. We are confident that our people are aligned to the most appropriate Craft Community. That does not mean that you are expected to be an expert in your new community. You may have been selected for a particular community because you represent a different, but necessary, perspective. If you have a question about your Craft Community alignment, you should reach out to your community leader or your craft talent partner.

Q: Can a member of a Craft engage in work that is not directly related to their Craft Community?

Yes. Craft Communities are a dedicated space for belonging and development — they are intended to be communities. They are not intended to narrow or limit opportunities to work on projects or to create silos. For example, if someone is part of the brand design & content Craft Community, they can still work on a digital platform project, just as someone in the products and platform Craft Community can work on brand projects. Fluidity of learning and cross-craft collaboration are encouraged and expected.

Q: How will the reorganization create greater collaboration and cross-craft fertilization?

Aligning our organization around client needs and talent expertise increases our ability to deploy the right team and talents to the right client work at the right moment. We invite you to lean into the opportunity to work with, learn from, and get to know your colleagues at a global level and across crafts.

Q: How will we navigate different creative points of view? Who will have a final say on the work?

One of the KPIs for the Craft Pods is quality of work. This means that they will be responsible for driving our creative and work standards, and for ensuring that whatever goes out into the world is of the highest standard. Part of this responsibility also includes working with Team Design to identify the right talent and matching them to the right opportunities so they can shine through the work.

THE PRODUCT PODS

Q: What is the role of the Product Pods?

The Product Pods are accountable for selling our soon-to-be-launched products to new and existing clients, alongside strategic product development and product quality assurance. Our new product offerings will unlock greater speed, consistency, quality, and overall value for our organization.

Q: How is the Product Pod organized?

Product Pods are organized around our clients' business challenges and mirror the three 'doors,' also referenced as 'gateways to growth,' we identified earlier this year: Experience Transformation, Technology Realization, and Growth Creation.

Q: Who are the leaders/point people within the Product Pods?

Lisa De Bonis is our CPO and leads the Product Pod. She is supported by Matt Creer, who oversees Product Pod operations & solutions, and Patrick Deere, who oversees Product Pod commercial finance.

Each Product Pod has been designed to appeal to our core client archetypes, which are the CMO/CXO in a disrupted industry; the CIO/CTO at a legacy organization in a disrupted industry; and the CEO/CXO in a mature or legacy category.

Q: Will members of the Product Pods get to work with clients?

Yes. Product Pod members will engage with clients as part of the product sales and implementation process, and, like all Pod leaders, will be accountable for retention and growth on one critical Top 50 global client relationship.

Q: How can I join the Product Pod in the future?

At the moment, the Product Pod represents only 1% of Huge, and the current vision is to keep this team small and flat. But we will listen carefully to the needs of the market and our people, and will evolve and adapt our approach as needed. If we determine over the next few months that team size is not right, and we need more support in the Product Pod, we will make sure to communicate this broadly, along with our process for being considered, in the appropriate channels.

HUGE HQ AND OPERATIONS-RELATED QUESTIONS

Q: What is Huge HQ?

The internal crafts that work together with our client-facing crafts and teams are now called Huge HQ. These crafts include DE&I, Growth, Operations, Finance, Accounting, Executive, Legal, Huge Habitats (formerly Real Estate), and Talent (which now includes Huge Experiences, the former Workplace team). Team Design (formerly Resource Management) and Recruiting, as well as Organizational Development & Effectiveness (formerly L&D), are all also part of Talent. IT is a part of Finance.

Q: Why did we rename Resource Management to Team Design, and the Workplace team to Huge Experiences?

Renaming both Resource Management and the Workplace team reflect that we are reimagining and recreating their remits to better serve our mission and new operational model. Our Team Design group is not charged with simply managing resources. Their charge is to partner with the Craft and Client Pods to design teams that will move people and brands to do huge things in the world. Similarly, our Huge Experiences team is dedicated to creating meaningful experiences for all of us, whether we are together or collaborating remotely.

Q: What changes will be made to the resourcing process to support successful implementation of our new organizational model? And is there a system in place for indexing current employee skills and capabilities within the Craft Pod, so they can be mapped to project needs globally?

As part of our growth model, we have built an extensive library of skills aligned to each craft and are mapping those skills and capabilities to each of our products. This skill mapping will support:

- Continued seamless and effective team design
- Clear identification of areas for skill mastery
- Clearer alignment of skills and capabilities to real opportunities, to gain experience leveraging those skills on our products

Additionally, we will be exploring an enterprise tool that will allow us to map skills to client needs systematically and at scale.

Q: Which Pods own job requisitions now?

In most circumstances in our new model, the Client Pod identifies the need for requisitions based on work a client has committed to do with Huge. Our Team Design group works with both the Client Pod and the Craft Pod to identify if the req can be filled by an existing Craft Pod member. If that is not possible, then Recruiting and the respective Craft will fill the req through external recruiting, in consultation with finance and operations.

Q: What selection criteria did the company employ to select its Client Pod, Craft Pod, Product Pod, and Craft Community leaders? What lenses were used to ensure diversity, equity, and inclusion in the process?

The executive leadership team selected leaders for the Client Pod, Craft Pod, and Product Pod from the existing pool of leaders within the company, and their selections were based on the employee's background, skills, relationships with current clients, and ability to lead teams. Several key steps were taken to aid in an equitable selection process and mitigate bias, including use of a common Craft Community definition; a consistent framework for Craft Community leader capability requirements; and ensuring that multiple leaders were involved in the selection process. Additionally, all executive leadership team members have bias disruption guide sheets for their ongoing use and have completed an executive DE&I workshop this year.

Q: Are we satisfied with the DE&I makeup of the global leadership team across the Client Pod, Craft Pod, Product Pod, and Huge HQ?

We have consistently believed that our work towards being a diverse and antiracist company is 'Never Done.' With that in mind, no, we are not satisfied with the DE&I makeup of the company. We continue our commitment to staying accountable and being held accountable for making progress across all levels, including leadership, at Huge. We recognize there is much work to do to ensure that we have a diverse talent pool at every level of the organization.

Q: Have we sunsetted any previously existing practices/disciplines/sub-crafts as part of this reorganization?

No capability or area of expertise is being sunsetted. Some capabilities are being combined under a single craft or Craft Community to reflect the breadth of our capabilities and align with our strategy. Examples of this would be:

- Content Strategy, Connections Strategy, Planning, and parts of Business Strategy are now within the Experience Strategy Craft Community
- Brand Design, Integrated, and Editorial are now within the Brand Design & Content Craft Community or the Experience Innovation Craft Community
- Strategic Communications is moving to Growth and merged with Huge Communications, and is now the Reputation & Communications Craft Community

Q: Can the reorganization sustain our current number of employees?

Yes. The company adapted our business to manage against global economic headwinds back in July 2022. We do not anticipate further reductions in headcount as part of the company's global reorganization.

Q: In practical terms, what does it mean to be a global organization? Will that change what I work on or who I work with?

By evolving into a truly global team, we are able to collaborate on a far greater range of efforts and products, and tap the full spectrum of talent that resides within Huge. Geography no longer artificially impedes professional growth, skill development, or work experience.

Q: Huge has tried to implement 'global' processes before. Why is this time different?

In the words of Andy Grove, former Chairman and CEO of Intel, "To understand a company's strategy, look at what they actually do rather than what they say they will do." To successfully implement consistent global processes, we first must engage in the hard work of transforming Huge into one globally-connected company. Our new organizational structure, new processes, and new accountabilities will enable us to walk the walk and talk the talk.

Q: What is the process for implementing these changes, and when will they take effect?

The broad organizational design changes are effective immediately. However, in keeping with our guiding principle of minimizing disruption, we will transition some meetings and practices over time. For example, we will be thoughtful in the timing as we sunset regional-based activities and introduce the corresponding activities within the new structure (e.g., Team Design meetings, regional all-hands sessions, etc.).

Q: Is there a new company-wide team organization chart available?

Yes. You can view the new org chart online.

Q: How will we know if the reorg is successful? What KPIs are leadership attaching to this reorganization?

Quite simply, our people and business will grow. Beyond the contents of a balance sheet, we will understand that we are succeeding as we listen to our people, invest in their growth, and see our client relationships deepen. That said, we have identified a number of KPIs that specifically relate to the remits of a given Pod, which will be measured and monitored on a regular basis, with reporting structures to match.

Client Pod KPIs:
- Client success (i.e., business outcomes)
- Client revenue and retention
- Client and team satisfaction

Craft Pod KPIs:
- Quality of work
- Client results (i.e., sales volume)
- Employee engagement

Product Pod KPIs:
- Product sales
- Product training
- Product quality (i.e., promised outcomes)

Q: Who defines 'success' on a project or within a product?

The client. As a client-centric organization, we need to be united in our belief that our success will be dependent on whether the work we do helps our client achieve their desired outcomes, and whether they are satisfied with the quality of our craft and their experience collaborating with us in pursuit of those outcomes. Beyond that, we have a detailed list of KPIs for the Client Pod, Product Pod, and Craft Pod members to determine success unique to their respective place in the structure of the company. But the client is the ultimate tiebreaker.

Q: Have clients been notified of the changes we're making?

This is an internal reorganization that will not affect most of our clients. In certain situations, where a client now has a new Executive Sponsor, we will manage that transition carefully, and ensure that those clients are introduced to the Client Pod president now accountable for their business.

Q: What client expectations will need to be set to support this new structure?

For clients with whom we have long-running relationships, it will be business as usual. Based on our 'minimum disruption' principle, virtually nothing will change in day-to-day activity. That said, if Client Partners perceive that our new product suite would either help open doors to clients with whom we do not have a relationship, or deepen existing relationships, then they will be encouraged to include our new product suite in their bi-annual Client Partnership plans. These clients will also know that they will now have access to Huge talent from around the world — a material benefit to their businesses.

For newer and less tenured clients, our Client Partner, Growth team, and Client Pod presidents will partner with Product Pod leads to identify opportunities to bring new products forward, on a case-by-case basis. We will be sharing that process with the Client Partner and Growth teams, as well as with Client Pod leadership teams. (This was done in September 2022).

Q: Will we begin working with clients based in markets where we currently don't have offices or talent hubs?

Our global reorganization grants us significantly more flexibility to work with clients, regardless of where they're headquartered, where we have physical offices, and where we have talent density. If the right opportunity presents itself, we will collaborate with clients in regions and markets where we do not have a physical office location and where we do not currently have talent hubs.

Q: Which stage of the transformation does this reorganization mark?

Our transformation will be an iterative journey with a number of exciting dimensions. It includes this initial step of reorganizing our people to work globally and deliver our strategy. It will also include evolving our processes and systems over time, as well as the launch of products, which will form an integral part of our future.

Q: What are the remaining transformation stages, and what is the timing for each stage?

The rollout of our new products will be a key milestone of our transformation. This product launch and its underlying commercial model are in final design stages, and we have already begun to pilot some of our products with both new and existing clients. More details about our products will be shared at the first post-reorganization all-hands meeting. (Note: This was done in September 2022.)

HOW THIS WILL IMPACT ME

Q: How will this change my day-to-day work?

We are all now a part of a global network, which means that we have access to an entire cohort of skills and competencies across the network that we can tap into, leverage, and learn from. The day-to-day activity for a significant majority of us will not change, but you will see new processes, toolkits, and enhancements to our current systems and tools.

Q: If I currently work on a retainer-based client, will that go away under our new operating model?

In keeping with our principle of minimum disruption, if you are currently working on retained business, you will continue to do so. Like everyone else, you will put your craft into practice within the Client Pod and you will be a member of a Craft Community. If you are on retainer for a prolonged period of time, and would like to cycle out to work on new clients or projects, please alert your manager and Team Design partner, who will make every effort to accommodate your request. In addition, working on a retainer client will not prevent you from being brought on to new clients or projects if your skills are a match, and a responsible transition is facilitated to 'do no harm' to the existing client project and relationship.

Q: How will this reorganization help me do better work or gain new skills?

This opportunity only begins with the reorg. As part of our transformation, we will be evolving processes to reduce friction in day-to-day work and delivery. Our new structure will enable you to learn from and get to know the full global team in your craft. Skills development across global teams can be deeper, richer, and more informed by the dialogues and organic connections that emerge among Craft Communities. And we will continue to invest in our organizational development capabilities, to ensure that our people develop the skills they need to deliver on our ambition.

Q: As a global organization, will salaries by level be consistent, regardless of where people live?

Our philosophy regarding base compensation has not changed as part of this reorganization. We will continue to base our salary ranges on local markets.

Q: Can I live and work from anywhere?

Our policies and processes regarding work locations have not changed since New World Working was announced. That policy can be referenced on our employee intranet.

Q: With regions going away and crafts consolidating, does this limit my opportunities for autonomy?

We believe this transformation will actually increase your opportunities for growth and autonomy. Opportunities will be available across the global organization, and regional alignment or a person's location will not constrain the scope or scale of opportunities our talent can pursue. Our new product offerings will create space in the business for more agency and more autonomy across all levels, and also create more opportunities to add both breadth and depth to your skills. Additionally, we have invested, and plan to continue to invest, in our organizational effectiveness, plus our learning and development capabilities.

Q: Does anyone's immediate supervisor/manager change with this reorganization?

Some manager changes have occurred, and will occur, as part of this reorganization. However, anyone whose manager is shifting immediately has already been notified of the change. Maintaining as many existing manager relationships as possible — provided that it made sense in the new organizational model — was a key principle in our change-management approach. In the future, manager changes may happen if they are deemed necessary to further align reporting relationships within the new organizational structure.

Q: Are Craft Pod managers still responsible for the onboarding, training and overall career growth of their direct reports?

Yes, managers should continue to focus on the onboarding, engagement, and career growth of their direct reports, through intentional mentorship and coaching. To enable this, we are building craft-specific onboarding plans and a Leadership at Huge training program that will roll out in the coming months.

Q: Updates used to occur at office-level meetings. How will we find out about new clients and upcoming projects?

In addition to global all-hands meetings, workshares and talent hub events, our Client Pods, Craft Pods, Product Pods, and Craft Communities will all hold regular meetings and updates. As part of these meetings, participants will find out about new clients and upcoming projects. While we know that many people appreciated office and regional meetings, we are confident that the Pods will quickly institute their own rituals and meeting styles.

Q: Are there any job title or career path changes associated with this reorganization?

Some title changes have occurred, and will occur, to build consistency within a Craft or Craft Community. However, the scope of those roles has not shifted. Our full career architecture will clearly outline the progression of titles within each Craft. Vertical career paths will see little to no change, outside of the adoption of extended individual contributor career tracks and a clear differentiation into a manager career track. This transformation, underpinned by our shift to a global, craft-based model, will actually introduce more career opportunities as the full, global career lattice at Huge will be available.

Q: If my title or role changes, am I entitled to a raise?

Any title or role changes are part of the organizational change and do not equate to promotions. As stated above, these changes build consistency and alignment with our new organizational model. The same criteria that would otherwise determine a raise or promotion still apply.

Q: Will Huge be providing new job descriptions and ways of working for any roles under the new organizational structure?

For roles that are newly created, KPIs and accountabilities have been defined. Additionally, as we finalize our updated career architecture, growth models and KPIs will be rolled out to the organization.

Q: Will we need to adopt new skills or trades as part of this reorganization?

Our people development philosophy continues to be grounded in a blended growth model inclusive of your career aspirations, strengths, development needs, and the needs of our business. The opportunity to develop breadth in your skills, and acquire new skills, will exist for everyone at Huge, as will the opportunity to deepen your existing skills. As we introduce new products and strategies, relevant training will be provided to build familiarity and comfort with these offerings.

Q: How will teams be designed globally? How will Team Design know my capabilities and how to deploy me?

Teams will be designed globally based on employees' skills and best fit for work. In many cases, your Team Design partners will not change. But to ensure that we thoroughly understand the best way to cast teams, we will be sending out a survey to all employees where you can share your professional aspirations, experiences, and goals. In addition, you can expect a 1:1 meeting with your Team Design partner. (Note: these meetings were conducted in the fourth quarter of 2022.)

Q: What guardrails will be put in place to support a healthy work/life balance for those working on projects with team members spread across multiple time zones?

Becoming a truly global organization will create more opportunities for us to design diverse teams across our entire network. While there may be some early challenges associated with working across multiple time zones, we believe that by offering a flexible working model, combined with flexible hours and open communication with our teams and managers, we all can maintain a healthy work/life balance while creating the career-defining experiences we want. Our Program Delivery, Operations, and Talent teams are experts in building strong asynchronous work environments and will work to establish the right team norms at the beginning of each project.

NOTES

1. Aaron Shapiro, 2005–2018; Michael Koziol, 2018–2019; Pete Stein, 2019–2020; Raj Singhal, 2020–2021; Mat Baxter, 2021-today.

2. https://adage.com/article/special-report-book-of-tens-2011/ten-marketing-books-read/231470

3. https://investors.interpublic.com/news-releases/news-release-details/interpublic-acquire-stake-huge

4. https://adage.com/article/agency-news/founders-digital-shop-huge-depart/146431

5. https://adage.com/article/agency-news/founders-digital-shop-huge-depart/146431

6. *Living Large: The World of Harold Mitchell*, Harold Mitchell, Melbourne University Publishing, 2009.

7. *Naked: The numbers prove we were right to do the Witchery jacket hoax*, Mumbrella, Tim Burrowes, January 29, 2009, https://mumbrella.com.au/naked-the-numbers-prove-we-were-right-to-do-the-witchery-jacket-hoax-1781.

8. *Adweek*, "Photon Acquires Naked," Steve McClellan, February 5, 2008.

9. *Adweek*, op. cit.

10. *Mumbrella*, "Naked Communications faces the sad fact that being clever doesn't make money anymore," August 26, 2015.

11. Toby Jenner continued his distinguished executive career, moving to Singapore, New York and London with Mediacom before becoming Global CEO of Wavemaker, one of WPP's major media agencies, in 2019.

12. *The Australian Financial Review Magazine*, "How IPG Mediabrands head Henry Tajer is reinventing Adland," Paul McIntyre, April 28, 2016.

13. *Mumbrella*, "Now Mat Baxter has signed on for the project, Henry Tajer's Entourage is complete," September 2, 2015, https://mumbrella.com.au/now-mat-baxter-has-signed-on-for-the-project-henry-tajers-entourage-is-complete-315582. The seven-member Australian 'Entourage' gang included Henry Tajer, Global CEO of Mediabrands; Mat Baxter, Global Chief Strategy and Creative Officer; Travis Johnson, Global Head of IPG Media Lab; Marc Lomas, SVP Programmatic at Cadreon (part of Mediabrands); Dianne Richardson, Chief Strategy Officer, UM Worldwide; and Charles Godbold, Global Head of Media Auditing.

14. RECMA was established in Paris in 1991 as an independent company that evaluates media agencies on a worldwide basis. It is an acronym that stands for Revue des Etudes Cooperatives, Mutualistes et Associatives (Research Company Evaluating the Media Agency Industry).

15. *Business Insider*, "Flashback: This Is What The First-Ever Website Looked Like," Alyson Shontell, June 29, 2011, bit.ly/3oFIWRO.

16. *Provoke Media*, "WPP Wins Global Dell Pitch, Will Build New Agency," Paul Holmes, December 3, 2007, https://www.provokemedia.com/latest/article/wpp-wins-global-dell-pitch-will-build-new-agency.

17. *Marketing Dive*, "Why Planet Fitness went from 16 agencies to one with new AOR Publicis," Chris Kelly, September 3, 2021.

18. *Just Auto*, "Bentley names new marketing agencies," Graeme Roberts, August 10, 2022.

19. Crafts at Huge include Client Executives (to be called Client Partners in the future), Strategists, Data Analysts, Program Delivery specialists, Project Managers, Technologists, and Creatives.

20. At the first executive retreat, Baxter and ELT agreed to abandon the term 'agency' for Huge.

21. *Cultish: The Language of Fanaticism*, Amanda Montell, Harper Wave, 2021.

22. *AdAge*, "Why Huge is Swapping Many of its Physical Offices for Experiences and Co-Working Spaces," Brian Bonilla, May 17, 2022.

23. The source of this supposed Jobs quotation is unknown. It is often referenced, and repeated in print. This instance came from Goodreads.com, https://www.goodreads.com/quotes/988332-some-people-say-give-the-customers-what-they-want-but.

24. *Marketing Management*, 15th Edition, Philip Kotler and Kevin Lane Keller, Pearson, 2016.

25. RACI is a system that defines who is Responsible, who is Accountable (having approval authority), who needs to be Consulted, and who needs to be Informed.

26. *The Structure of Scientific Revolutions*, Thomas S. Kuhn, University of Chicago Press, 1962.

27. See, for example, a plain-vanilla definition of paradigm shift in the Merriam-Webster Dictionary, which defines it as an important change that happens when the usual way of thinking about or doing something is replaced by a new and different way, https://www.merriam-webster.com/dictionary/paradigm%20shift.

28. https://www.space.com/17661-theory-general-relativity.html

29. See "'Nobody Knows Anything' About What Works in the Film Business. The Same is True About Marketing." Article in *Media Village*, Michael Farmer, May 11, 2021, https://bit.ly/3PFWl3k.

30. *The Structure of Scientific Revolutions*, Kuhn, op cit.

31. *The Structure of Scientific Revolutions*, Kuhn, op cit.

ACKNOWLEDGMENTS

This insider's view of Huge's transformation could not have been completed without the extraordinary openness and support of Mat Baxter and Huge's management team. Mat encouraged me to begin this task in 2021; henceforth, he and Tess Bricker ensured that I was invited to and given full access to in-person management retreats, Zoom management meetings and any current or historical data I asked for. They encouraged the members of Huge's executive leadership team to discuss the transformation and their management responsibilities openly and confidentially with me. Most importantly, they let me get on with my work without any efforts to shape the narrative or edit the outcome. As a fly on the wall, I was never brushed away or swatted. I was truly blessed with the degree of freedom I had while I completed the research and writing.

Consequently, *Madison Avenue Makeover* is my own work, and I take full responsibility for its structure, content and conclusions – including any errors or misstatements, which I hope are few.

That said, this work could not have been completed without the help of many fine friends and colleagues. At Huge, I owe a great debt to Mat Baxter, Tess Bricker, Aaron Washington, Adrienne Imbriaco, Alex Pym, Andrew Silver, Blake Wirht, Cara DiNorcia, Chris Wlach, Frisco Chau, Fura Johannesdottir, Jason Schlossberg, Jon Judah, Lisa De Bonis, Mark Manning, Martin Riley, Matt Creer, Matt Di Paola, Matt Weiss, Megan Malli, Mimi Moore, Patrick Burke, Ryan Ku, Toni Lowe and Urvashi Shivdasani. At IPG, Philippe Krakowsky and Tom Cunningham provided vital insights from the holding company perspective.

At The Business Model Company, Caroline Johnson was generous and open about TBMC's history, operations, practice and program with Huge. Chris Zook, my former colleague at Bain & Company and twenty-year head of Bain's strategy consulting practice was kind in agreeing to read the manuscript and write the foreword, giving us a strategy expert's view of Huge's business transformation.

I had the benefit of friends and colleagues who read early versions of the manuscript and gave me helpful advice and counsel. Thanks to Amy Armstrong, Bob Liodice, Professor Brian Sheehan, Brian Wieser, Christine Removille, Darren Woolley, Dennis Berger, Janet Lyons, Jeff McElnea, Jim Singer, Jim Stillman, Joanne Davis, John Seifert, Jon Bond, Kristen Simmons, Laurie Rosenfield, Marla Kaplowitz, Professor Nancy Tag, Rishad Tobaccowala, Robert Kearns, Professor Rodes Ponzer, Sabrina Traskos, Steve Farmer, Tim Williams, Tom Rosenwald and Tom Triscari, Additionally, I am grateful for the insights of Sasha Kirovski, who founded Huge in 1999 with David Skokna, and Mike Boyd and Adam Ferrier, who worked with Mat Baxter in Australia during Baxter's early career in media.

Dennis Flad contributed the cartoons for Chapters 1 through 14. Dennis is both a strategy consultant, living and operating in Switzerland, and a talented artist in his own right – he has the gift of working simultaneously with the left-side and the right-side of his brain. I'm grateful for Dennis' artistic contributions for this book.

Martin Liu, Clare Christian, Caroline Li and Teya Ucherdzhieva did extraordinary work at LID Publishing to design, edit and accelerate the publishing process so that the story of Huge's transformation could be released in a timely manner. Shona Baxter was instrumental in conceiving the original design for the cover – thank you, Shona!

Finally, my partner at home, Jo Ann Lynch, supported me every painful step of the way, tactfully ignoring my lapses in communication and attention. I was surely blessed by her understanding and support – I could not have done this book without her.